W9-BSM-262

WORLD WAR I
CHRONICLE OF AMERICA'S WARS

Ruth Tenzer Feldman

LERNER PUBLICATIONS COMPANY
MINNEAPOLIS

CHAPTER PHOTO CAPTIONS

Introduction: U.S. infantrymen fire a 37-mm gun at German troops in the Argonne Forest in 1918.

Chapter 1: Sarajevo police arrest Gavrilo Princip moments after he assassinated Archduke Franz Ferdinand of Austria in 1914.

Chapter 2: Soldiers unroll a spool of barbed wire around a newly built trench.

Chapter 3: *(From left to right)* Field Marshall von Hindenburg, Kaiser Wilhem II, and General Ludendorff meet at German general headquarters in January 1917.

Chapter 4: Phosphorous bombs explode during a night attack in France.

Chapter 5: U.S. Marines take aim from the trenches in Brouvannes, France, in February 1918.

Chapter 6: Near the Somme River, U.S. infantrymen advance through bursting German shells.

Chapter 7: French, British, and U.S. soldiers and medical workers celebrate armistice in November 1918.

Epilogue: During the 1920s, women known as flappers began to discard society's rules about how they should behave. Here, the Royal Order of Flappers holds a meeting.

Copyright © 2004 by Ruth Tenzer Feldman

All rights reserved. International copyright secured. No part of this book may be reproduced, stored in a retrieval system, or transmitted in any form or by any means—electronic, mechanical, photocopying, recording, or otherwise—without the prior written permission of Lerner Publications Company, except for the inclusion of brief quotations in an acknowledged review.

Lerner Publications Company
A division of Lerner Publishing Group
241 First Avenue North
Minneapolis, MN 55401

Website address: www.lernerbooks.com

Library of Congress Cataloging-in-Publication Data

Feldman, Ruth Tenzer.
    World War I / Ruth Tenzer Feldman.
      p.   cm.— (Chronicle of America's wars)
    Includes bibliographical references and index.
    Contents: 1. Entanglements—2. Widening war—3. Turning points—4. Over there—5. Over the top—6. Pershing's Army—7. Uneasy peace—8. Epilogue.
    ISBN: 0–8225–0148–1 (lib. bdg. : alk. paper)
    1. World War, 1914–1918—United States. 2. World War, 1914–1918—Campaigns—Western Front. 3. World War, 1914–1918—Causes. 4. United States—Foreign relations—1913–1921. 5. Neutrality—United States—History—20th century. 6. World War, 1914–1918—Peace. [1. World War, 1914–1918—United States. 2. World War, 1914–1918.] I. Title: World War 1. II. Title: World War One. III. Title. IV. Series.
D570.F45 2004
940.4'0973—dc22   2003018806

Manufactured in the United States of America
1 2 3 4 5 6 – JR – 09 08 07 06 05 04

TABLE OF CONTENTS

INTRODUCTION

France, October 2, 1918. Charles Whittlesey, a U.S. major, told his troops, "Our mission is to hold this position at all costs."

That day Whittlesey and his men were ordered to rout German troops from their heavily fortified trenches in the Argonne Forest in France. The Americans slipped through a gap in the German line and fought their way to an old mill by a pond in the Charlevaux ravine. By the time the troops reached the mill, 90 of them had been killed or wounded. They were down to a fighting force of about 550.

The men dug in near the mill and sent a message back to headquarters by carrier pigeon. They had brought machine guns, rifles, and plenty of ammunition but little food.

That night German troops strung barbed wire across the path the Americans had taken so other U.S. troops couldn't easily break through. Whittlesey and his men found themselves trapped in an oval-shaped area about 300 yards by 60 yards. This was roughly two and one-half times as long as a U.S. football field and about as wide.

The Germans attacked Whittlesey's men with machine gun and mortar fire and grenades for the next two days. Whittlesey sent off carrier pigeons asking for support, but no U.S. troops were able to get through. German snipers shot at every sound and movement made by the trapped Americans. Then, because of a terrible mistake in calculating Whittlesey's exact location, U.S. artillery began shelling Whittlesey's position.

Desperate after several hours of "friendly fire," Whittlesey sent out a carrier pigeon—likely his last—named Cher Ami (French for Dear Friend). Strapped to the pigeon's leg was this message: "We're along the road parallel 276.4. Our artillery is dropping a barrage directly on us. For heaven's sake, stop it."

Cher Ami had flown 11 missions and should have gone directly to headquarters. Instead, he landed on a nearby tree, perhaps overwhelmed by the shelling. Whittlesey and the pigeon keeper threw stones at him, and finally, Cher Ami left for his loft 25 miles away. There he collapsed with a shattered breastbone, a missing eye, and the message dangling from a ligament of his shot-off leg.

The U.S. friendly fire stopped. The next day, however, friendly French artillery mistakenly fired on Whittlesey's position. After that stopped, the Germans attacked. Still, the men fought on. U.S. planes flew over, dropping supplies of food and ammunition. Not one package made it to Whittlesey's men. German soldiers had a great dinner.

U.S. newspapers published stories about what they called the Lost Battalion, even though Whittlesey commanded men from two battalions and they weren't lost. Allied troops certainly knew their general location.

October 6 saw more fighting. U.S. planes finally attacked the German forces, but still the men were trapped. That night the Lost Battalion took rifles and ammunition from dead Germans to use the next day. Whittlesey and Captain George McMurtry, his second in command, were both wounded.

On October 7, Private Lowell Hollingshead and several others left the area—it's not clear on whose orders. That evening Hollingshead returned with a typed message. He had been captured but refused to give information. The German officer in charge, who had lived in the United States, wrote a courteous note about Hollingshead and added this:

> The suffering of your wounded men can be heard here in the German lines, and we are appealing to your humane sentiments to stop. A white flag shown by one of your men will tell us that you agree to these conditions.

Whittlesey simply ordered his men to hide the white panels for signaling airplanes. Having lasted this long, he refused to surrender.

Meanwhile, Private Abraham Krotoshinsky, one of the volunteers who had crawled through the enemy lines to get help, had not returned. At one point, he lay hidden in bushes so close to the enemy that a German officer stepped on his fingers. "I managed to stay quiet, but it took a great deal of effort," he said.

Hours later, Krotoshinsky was able to zigzag toward headquarters. That night he stumbled into a trench. He thought he heard American voices, but he lacked one vital piece of information—the password of the day. There were no choices left. With his last strength, Krotoshinsky shouted "Hello! Hello!" Frustrating no-win battles and agonizing human suffering like that of the Lost Battalion characterized the four years of global conflict known as World War I.

ENTANGLEMENTS

Charles Whittlesey and his men found themselves trapped in the Argonne Forest partly because a Serb named Gavrilo Princip had a second chance. Here's how.

Over the centuries before World War I, different rulers in Europe gained power and then lost it. National borders changed. In 1914 Hungary was partly under the rule of the Austrian emperor. The vast empire of Austria-Hungary controlled neighboring Bosnia-Herzegovina. Serbia, another neighbor, was fiercely independent. Some Serbs who were living in Austria-Hungary also wanted independence.

In June 1914, Austrian troops held training exercises in Bosnia. Austria's Archduke Franz Ferdinand attended them because he was the army's inspector general. Ferdinand was also the nephew of Austria's Emperor, Franz Josef. When the exercises were over, Ferdinand and his wife, Sophie, visited Bosnia-Herzegovina's capital, Sarajevo.

Their visit was on June 28, the anniversary of the defeat of the Serbs by the Turks in 1389 and the beginning of more than 500 years of oppressive foreign rule. Although Serbia had recently gained independence from Turkey, Ferdinand knew it was a dangerous day to be in Sarajevo. Sure enough, a group of four Serbs and one Bosnian threw a bomb at the archduke's car. One of the Serbs was a 19-year-old named Gavrilo Princip. The bomb bounced off the archduke's car and exploded under the car following it.

Later that day, Ferdinand decided to visit a man injured by the explosion. The assassins continued to lurk along the main streets of the city. Gavrilo Princip was nearby. He had his second chance at the archduke when the driver of the archduke's car stopped after taking a wrong turn and began to back up. Princip stepped up to within five feet of the car and fired several shots, killing Ferdinand and his wife.

By July 2, Princip and the others were caught. Although Austrian subjects, they were given their weapons in Serbia and had been smuggled across the border by a Serbian organization determined to free Bosnia-Herzegovina from Austria-Hungary and unite it with Serbia.

MISTAKES LEAD TO MISTAKES

Some political officials in Austria-Hungary wanted Emperor Franz Josef to act quickly against Serbia. They believed that other European nations would not come to Serbia's aid as long as Austria-Hungary did not try to take control of that independent country.

But the emperor of Austria and prime minister of Hungary were cautious. They did not want to act against Serbia without the support of Germany, which had a treaty with Austria-Hungary. Serbia was under the protection of Russia, and Russia had military treaties with France and Britain.

Austria-Hungary's unwillingness to act alone made a local problem larger. On July 5, an Austrian official met with Wilhelm II, kaiser (ruler) of Germany. The kaiser didn't think that France and Russia would get involved. He announced that Germany would support Austria-Hungary, then left for a three-week cruise of Norway's fjords (deep

Kaiser Wilhelm II

ocean inlets). Other officials also were on vacation and communication was slow. The next three weeks were filled with political blunders.

On July 23, Austria-Hungary delivered a note to Serbia, Russia, Germany, Britain, and France. The note demanded that Serbia control terrorist actions. It also included a provision for Austria-Hungary to supervise the arrest and questioning of Serbian officials who might be supporting the terrorists. Serbia had 48 hours to respond.

Serbia's ministers were just about to agree to Austria-Hungary's demands. Then, on July 25, they learned that Czar Nicholas II, who ruled Russia, might support his "little slavic brothers in Serbia." Nicholas II began readying his army and, as required under a treaty, notified France he was doing so. With this support from Russia, Serbia decided to reject several of the note's demands. On July 28, Austria-Hungary declared war on Serbia.

At that time, most nations in Europe were ruled by royal families who were related to each other. On July 29, the kaiser of Germany sent a telegram—in English—to his cousin the czar of Russia. The kaiser urged him to help smooth over the situation between the warring nations. The czar at first scaled back preparations for the war, then ordered full-scale readiness.

Germany's military officials told the kaiser that it was important for Germany to mobilize (prepare its military) too. The German army

Family Squabble

Kaiser Wilhelm II of Germany, Czar Nicholas II of Russia, and King George V of England were all cousins. The correspondence between cousins Wilhelm and Nicholas became known as the "Willy-Nicky Letters." Years before, their grandmother, Queen Victoria of England, had believed that the international marriages of her children and grandchildren would help keep the world at peace. How wrong she was!

had a long-standing plan to avoid fighting wars in both the east and west at the same time. It was called the Schlieffen Plan in honor of the man who devised it in the 1890s. The first plan called for German forces to march westward and invade Belgium, then France, in order to win there. Then they could turn their forces to Russia in the east.

Committed by treaty to defend Russia, France started to mobilize on July 31. Germany began to mobilize that same day. It declared war on Russia on August 1. The kaiser wanted his army to march eastward, against Russia. He wanted to cancel the Schlieffen Plan. But his advisers said they needed one year to come up with a new plan. There wasn't time. So Germany demanded that Belgium—a neutral country—allow German forces to invade in order to reach France, an ally of Russia. Belgium refused.

Germany then declared war on France and Belgium. Britain and France had a treaty to protect the neutrality of Belgium. Britain demanded that Germany halt its invasion of Belgium. When Germany did not reply by midnight on August 4, Britain declared war on Germany. The next day, Austria-Hungary joined Germany and declared war on Russia. The Great War, as it would soon be called, had begun.

Most Europeans thought the war would be over soon. All across the continent, trains brought hundreds of thousands of men and horses toward the battle lines. Troop departures were treated like a holiday.

French, British, and Russian troops were called the Allied Forces, or Allies. Germany and Austria-Hungary were called the Central Powers. Italy had a treaty with the Central Powers but declared itself neutral.

German troops parade past celebrating crowds in Berlin on their way to the front (zone of conflict between armies). Before the war had truly begun, many people felt that it would be quick and painless.

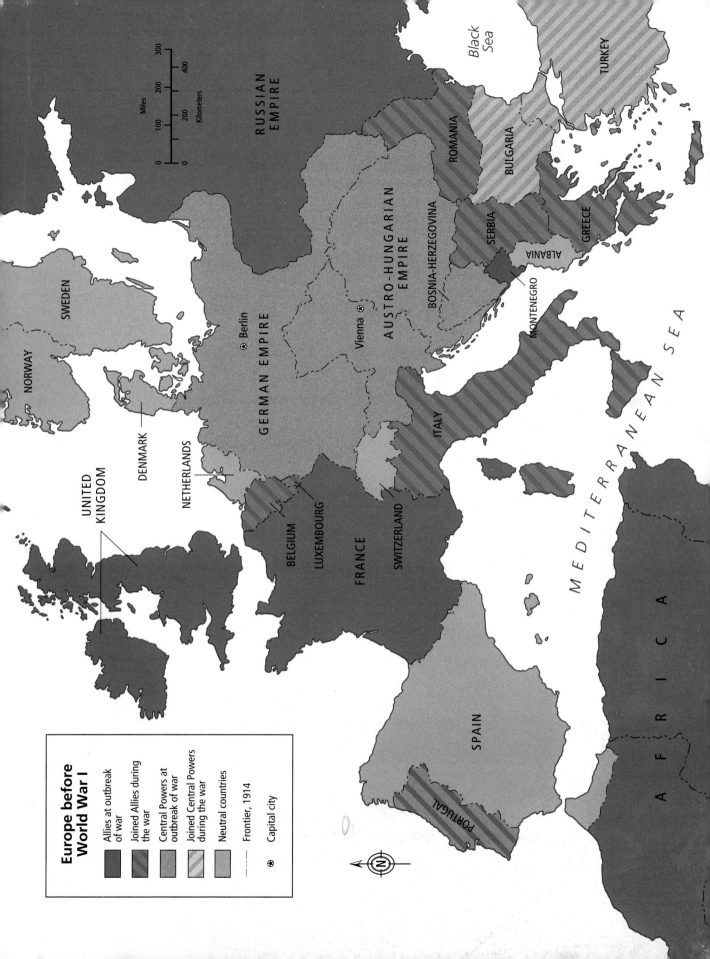

Europe before World War I

Allies at outbreak of war
Joined Allies during the war
Central Powers at outbreak of war
Joined Central Powers during the war
Neutral countries

Frontier, 1914

⊛ Capital city

Miles
Kilometers
300
400
200
200
100
100
0
0

N

Black Sea

MEDITERRANEAN SEA

RUSSIAN EMPIRE

TURKEY

BULGARIA

ROMANIA

SERBIA

GREECE

ALBANIA

MONTENEGRO

BOSNIA-HERZEGOVINA

AUSTRO-HUNGARIAN EMPIRE

Vienna ⊛

GERMAN EMPIRE

⊛ Berlin

ITALY

SWEDEN

NORWAY

DENMARK

NETHERLANDS

UNITED KINGDOM

BELGIUM

LUXEMBOURG

FRANCE

SWITZERLAND

SPAIN

PORTUGAL

AFRICA

Poison Gas

France, not Germany, was the first country to use vaporized chemicals (gas) against enemy troops in World War I. In August 1914, they fired the first tear-gas grenades (xylyl bromide) against the Germans. In January 1915, Germany first used tear gas against Russian armies, but the gas turned to liquid in the cold air.

In April 1915, Germany was the first to use poisonous chlorine gas, which causes fluid to collect in the lungs. Britain, then France, followed suit. Both sides also used phosgene gas. Like chlorine gas, phosgene gas

Later in the war, gas masks became a part of standard issue uniforms for soldiers on both sides. Many men suffered chronic (ongoing) illness after gas attacks.

caused its victims to cough and choke. Phosgene was more potent, and a mixture of the two was even more harmful. In 1917 Germany started using mustard gas (yperite), an odorless chemical that caused blisters inside the body and on the skin. About 18 other gases were used as well.

Gas was used mainly in the west, where canisters were placed in mortars and hurled at the enemy trenches. Relatively few gas victims died, but many were sick the rest of their lives. The first gas masks were poorly made. Soldiers were told in an emergency to simply hold a urine-soaked cloth over their faces. By 1918 gas masks with filter respirators usually provided effective protection.

Belgium had spent money to build forts to protect its neutrality, but the Belgian army was no match for German troops. Although few Belgian civilians (non-military citizens) fought against the invasion, Germans killed many of them and burned their towns. The worst attack began on August 25 in the university town of Louvain. German troops burned the university's 230,000-book library, destroyed 1,100 other buildings, killed 209 civilians, and evacuated 42,000 others by force.

One reason for what the Allies soon called the "rape of Belgium" was the Schlieffen Plan. The plan called for a massive show of force leading to a quick victory in a short war. But the French also had a military plan, called Plan XVII. Plan XVII called for bringing as many troops forward as fast as possible to meet a German invasion on all fronts. And that's exactly what France did—with the aid of British troops.

French armies in the south and central part of France rushed to meet the advancing Germans. British troops crossed the English Channel and rushed into northern Belgium.

The massive, mechanized German army swept through Belgium and advanced toward Paris, the capital of France. In early September, the Allies were finally able to stop the Germans in a battle near the Marne River, east of Paris.

By the end of September 1914, it was clear the Schlieffen Plan and Plan XVII had failed. The Great War would not be over with a quick victory for either side. Both sides dug trenches to protect themselves from enemy fire. They surrounded their trenches with barbed wire and set up rows of machine guns.

The first major battle after trenches were established took place near the town of Ypres in Flanders, in the northern part of Belgium. British forces held their ground there against the Germans for a week in October. About 250,000 soldiers died at Ypres.

Shortly after the battle of Ypres, Turkey joined the Central Powers. This made it almost impossible for the Allies to ship supplies to Russian ports on the Black Sea. The only way to reach these ports was through a narrow water passage controlled by Turkey.

In just the few months since the Great War started, the Allies and Central Powers had built a continuous, 475-mile-long line of trenches facing each other from the North Sea to Switzerland. They were caught in a mutual trap. This would be a war of attrition, meaning that both sides would continue fighting until one side lost the most men or was so worn down that it

A frostbitten British soldier picks at his meal in the trenches. The trench system was vital to both sides in protecting soldiers. But life in the trenches was dirty, cold, and miserable.

couldn't afford to send supplies to them. This would take a long time and cause millions of deaths.

THE UNITED STATES IN 1914

The United States was struggling with social changes in 1914. U.S. industries were expanding, yet the economy suffered from its worst depression (downturn) in about 20 years. Many of the recent immigrants to the United States were extremely poor. Cities were overcrowded and polluted. Thousands of children died from disease and malnutrition.

In April 1914, U.S. president Woodrow Wilson tried to restore a more democratic government to Mexico after a military dictator took control there. U.S. Marines landed at the Mexican port of Veracruz,

claiming that Mexican troops did not salute American vessels entering Mexican ports. More than 400 people were killed or wounded in the clash. The only result was that the dictator became more popular among Mexicans.

That same month, in Ludlow, Colorado, the Colorado National Guard attacked a tent camp set up by miners who were striking to protest terrible working conditions. Guardsmen fired on the camp with machine guns and later burned it down, killing 10 adults and 11 children. Thousands demonstrated against what was called the Ludlow Massacre. President Wilson sent federal (U.S.) troops to occupy most of Colorado to restore order.

American manners and morals were changing too. In the cities, women were

Members of the Colorado National Guard prepare to move in on the striking miners of Ludlow, Colorado, in April 1914.

beginning to demand the right to vote. They stopped wearing tight-fitting corsets. They cut their hair short and wore ankle-revealing dresses. Alcohol and opium addiction were on the rise. Also on the rise were segregation laws and customs that kept African Americans second-class citizens.

When Britain declared war on Germany on August 4, President Woodrow Wilson was at the bedside of his dying wife, Ellen Axson Wilson. She died on August 6. Wilson thought that Europe was stuck with ancient ideas of empire and greed. He wanted the young democracy of the United States to stay out of the fighting and show a "true spirit of neutrality." In keeping with this policy, the Department of State refused to approve any loans or credits from American banks to the warring nations.

On August 15, 1914, the first ship sailed from the Atlantic to the Pacific Ocean through the Panama Canal, which France began and the United States completed. Comparing the events in Europe and Panama, the *New York Times* boasted: "The European ideal bears its full fruit of ruin and savagery [in war] just at the moment when the American ideal lays before the world a great work of peace, goodwill and fair play [the opening of the canal]."

At that time, more than one-third of Americans came from another country or had at least one foreign-born parent. Most Americans agreed with President Wilson that the United States should stay out of the war in Europe. But they worried about friends and relatives still living in "the old country." American charities, such as the

U.S. president Woodrow Wilson strongly believed that the United States should remain neutral in the Great War.

Committee for the Relief of Belgium, raised money and collected supplies to help civilians caught up in the conflict. U.S. secretary of state William Jennings Bryan tried to settle the European dispute through "cooling off" treaties. His efforts failed.

Meanwhile, President Wilson mourned deeply for his wife. He confided to Edward "Colonel" House, his personal adviser, that he "did not think straight any longer and had no heart for the things he was doing." By the end of 1914, as the slaughter in Europe continued, Wilson had decided that he was no longer fit to be president.

WIDENING WAR

2

While President Wilson wondered about his ability to remain in office, Jane Addams knew exactly what she wanted for America—peace. In January 1915, Addams led a political party that later became the Women's International League for Peace and Freedom. She met with Wilson several times and urged him to negotiate a settlement of the Great War.

Meanwhile, European nations realized how important U.S. industry and manpower could be in deciding which side would win. Modern warfare was an economic contest as well as a military one. Both the Allies and the Central Powers pressured the United States to lend them money and credit with which to buy supplies. The U.S. government reversed its policy and allowed trade with the warring nations.

Britain signed an agreement to buy weapons and supplies with money lent by the U.S. financial giant J. P. Morgan and Company. U.S. companies were also allowed to trade with the Central Powers, but trading with Germany was difficult. The British navy set up a blockade of Germany and laid mines in German ports. This prevented German vessels from leaving German ports and prevented ships from other countries from entering them. The blockade was against international law, and it caused great misery for the people of Germany, deprived of food and fuel.

In retaliation against the blockade, Germany decided to change the rules of war. On February 14, 1915, Germany declared that the water surrounding Britain was a war zone. Any ships there would be open to attack by an *unterseeboot* (undersea boat or submarine), or U-boat, for short.

Germany had only 21 U-boats at the start of 1915. They were frail and slow, hardly able to control the hundreds of ships steaming from U.S. ports. The submarines could slip through the British minefields, though, and at least threaten Allied shipping. How much of a threat was unclear. Americans knew very little about submarines at that time. They soon found out.

War in the trenches to the west of Germany in France and Belgium—the Western Front—was at a standstill. About two million Belgian, British, and French troops faced about two million German troops. But by the spring of 1915, the Great War had spread elsewhere. Italy joined the Allies and began fighting in southern Europe to gain territory belonging to Austria. In eastern Europe, Russian troops faced soldiers from Germany and Austria-Hungary. Soldiers from Britain, Australia, and New Zealand attacked Turkey in an effort to open up a supply route to Russia through the Black Sea. Turkish and Allied soldiers fought on the Gallipoli Peninsula

A damaged German U-boat surfaces off the Danish coast. U-boats were to become a symbol of the German military for members of the Allied forces.

Soldiers from Australia and New Zealand, a combined force called **ANZAC**, charge the enemy at Gallipoli, Turkey.

in Turkey for months. Finally, the Allies withdrew, after about 250,000 Allied soldiers were killed or injured. At least 90,000 Turks died as well.

Meanwhile, more than 1,000 women, including Jane Addams and other Americans, attended the International Congress of Women in the Netherlands. The women hoped to bring about negotiations for peace. They failed, and Addams returned home to a country closer to war.

THE *LUSITANIA*

On May 7, 1915, a German U-boat attacked the British luxury ocean liner, the *Lusitania*. Nearly 2,000 people were on board the *Lusitania* when it left New York for England. Germany had posted warnings in U.S. newspapers that the ship might be attacked when it entered enemy waters. Only one person canceled the trip.

The *Lusitania* was a huge ocean liner with 192 coal-burning furnaces. It was

likely carrying weapons for Britain, as well as its 2,000 passengers. A German U-boat fired a single torpedo at it, when the ship was about 10 miles off the coast of Ireland. Explosions rocked the ship and the *Lusitania* sank within minutes. Even the U-boat captain was shocked: "It was the most terrible sight I have ever seen."

About 1,200 passengers died, including 128 American men, women, and children. These were not the first American civilians killed at sea by Germany since the war began. But the loss of so many innocent lives enraged many Americans.

President Wilson continued his policy of neutrality. Three days after the *Lusitania* sank, he told the American people, "There is such a thing as a man being too proud to fight. There is such a thing as a nation being so right that it does not need to convince others by force that it is right."

Some Americans liked Wilson's speech. Others said it was too timid. America's

The ocean liner *Lusitania* was torpedoed by a German U-boat.

political leaders were also divided. Secretary of State William Jennings Bryan argued that Britain should partially lift its blockade of Germany to let fuel and medical supplies get through. In 1915 the number of German civilians dying from disease and starvation as a result of the British blockade was about 200 a day. Wilson sent a strongly worded protest to Germany about the sinking of the *Lusitania*. But he did not pressure Britain to even partially lift the blockade. Secretary of State Bryan resigned in protest. Wilson chose Robert Lansing to take Bryan's place.

Other political leaders also pressed for peace. One of the most vocal was Robert La Follette, a senator from Wisconsin. La Follette and others in his Progressive Party wanted the United States to concentrate on economic and political reforms at home, rather than fighting in battles overseas. William Taft, who had been president of the United States from 1909 to 1913, helped to establish the League to Enforce Peace. The league was the first group in the United States to promote an international peacekeeping organization.

However, an increasing number of Americans thought the country should prepare for war. The leader of this group was Theodore Roosevelt, who had been president of the United States from 1901 to 1909. Both Roosevelt and Taft had run against Wilson in the 1912 presidential election and lost.

Roosevelt encouraged businessmen to attend special training camps to learn about military life. One of the first groups went to a camp in Plattsburg, New York, to study with U.S. Army officers. Soon other groups trained in military camps in what became known as the Plattsburg Movement. In 1915 and 1916, thousands of men joined the movement. Among them was a trim, 32-year-old lawyer from Massachusetts named Charles Whittlesey.

In August 1915, at about the time the first businessmen left for Plattsburg, two more Americans drowned when a German U-boat sank the British merchant (trading) ship *Arabic*. Germany apologized for the loss of American lives and pledged to stop attacking merchant or passenger ships without warning. In the meantime, the German navy increased production of a better submarine for warfare on the open sea.

During 1915 the war continued to widen. Bulgaria declared war on Serbia in

October 1915. The Allies tried to reach Serbia through a route from Thessaloníki, Greece, but the Bulgarians beat them back. German troops under General Paul von Hindenburg stopped the Russians from advancing on Germany's eastern front.

The year ended on a good note for the U.S. president, despite the war in Europe. On December 18, 1915, Wilson married Edith Bolling Galt, a widow he had met in the spring.

Shortly after the wedding, Wilson's top political adviser, Edward House, left on a secret mission to Europe. Sir Edward Grey, the British foreign secretary, had written to House that Britain might welcome the United States' involvement in establishing peace. House was determined to see what he could do. He spent several months with government officials in Europe negotiating for a peaceful settlement to the war. House and Lord Grey even discussed the possibility of U.S. entry into the war if an agreement could not be reached. But this was never acted upon.

TROUBLE WITH MEXICO

The Wilsons returned from their honeymoon to find that, in addition to the tensions with Europe, there were new hostilities with Mexico. Texas governor James Ferguson claimed that armed Mexicans were attacking people in his state, which had been part of Mexico before the Mexican-American War (1846–1848). Venustiano Carranza, the newest Mexican leader, blamed the raids on Pancho Villa, his political rival.

On January 11, 1916, Mexican bandits—likely Villa's men—dragged several Americans from a train in northern Mexico and

Supporters of Pancho Villa languish in an American prison.

killed them. The U.S. public was outraged, but President Wilson was as unwilling to wage war with Mexico as with Germany.

On February 21, nearly one million German soldiers attacked the area around Verdun, a town in northeastern France. After the Germans took the fort at Verdun, the French troops dug in and refused to surrender any more land. Verdun was a salient, a piece of land that juts out behind the main enemy line, on the Western Front. This made it difficult to defend. Still the French and Germans fought over Verdun for the next 10 months. More than 700,000 soldiers were wounded or killed there.

Shortly after the German attack on Verdun, Lindley Garrison, the U.S. secretary of war, argued for a powerful military buildup. Wilson rejected Garrison's plans and replaced Garrison with Newton Baker. Baker supported former president Taft's League to Enforce Peace.

But peace was increasingly hard to come by. Germany announced that, starting on March 1, it would again launch submarine attacks an all armed enemy ships. About a week later, Pancho Villa and 1,500 men attacked Colombus, New Mexico. They set fire to buildings and killed about a dozen people before U.S. troops chased them back across the border. Wilson finally ordered his brigadier general, John Pershing, and several thousand soldiers to pursue Villa into Mexico. Pershing's men joined forces with

John Pershing

Carranza's soldiers and advanced farther into Mexican territory.

On March 24, a German submarine sank the French steamer *Sussex* in the English Channel. Two more Americans died. The United States threatened to cut off diplomatic relations with Germany, a first step toward war. But U.S. public opinion did not fully support the Allies.

The Great War continued to spread. Allied forces, including Japan, Canada, South Africa, New Zealand, and Australia, conquered German colonies in Asia and Africa. Turkey laid siege to British troops near Baghdad, then under Turkish rule. On April 29, about 10,000 British soldiers, facing starvation, finally surrendered to the Turks.

On May 4, Germany responded to U. S. pressure after the sinking of the *Sussex*. Germany pledged to warn all merchant and passenger ships before attacking them. At the end of May, however, Germany and Britain fought the largest naval battle of the Great War. The German navy attempted to break the stranglehold the British blockade held over the North Sea. Germany claimed to have won the battle, since its navy lost fewer men and ships than the British navy. But Britain continued to control the Atlantic Ocean and maintain its blockade.

In addition to blockading German ports, Britain refused to buy anything from U.S. companies that traded with Germany. The United States was a neutral county. Therefore, it could supply both sides in the war. Britain's actions led to protests in the United States and even sabotage of supplies headed for Great Britain.

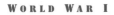

In the Trenches

Life in the trenches was at best boring, at worst deadly. Soldiers waited nervously between attacks, then faced the horror of watching a trench mate blown to bits by a grenade or shot by machine-gun fire. The bottoms of many trenches were covered with several inches of water from rain or ground seepage. The water was contaminated with blood, human waste, and bacteria from decaying flesh. Soldiers might be standing in water for days. Small cuts or blisters on the soldier's feet could develop into "trench foot," infections that killed or disabled them. Lice and rats were a constant hazard. Army units took turns manning the trenches and withdrawing into better conditions behind the front lines. A week or two in the trenches was the most a soldier could take.

The trench system on the Western Front included fire trenches—the front line of attack—and the support trenches behind. Some trench systems had elaborate, fortified underground rooms, called bunkers. In 1916 the German army constructed the Siegfried Line, which was a series of specially fortified trenches and bunkers. The Allies called these fortifications the Hindenburg Line, after the German general who designed it. The Hindenburg Line stretched along the northern and central parts of the Western Front. It was finally destroyed by Allied forces in 1918.

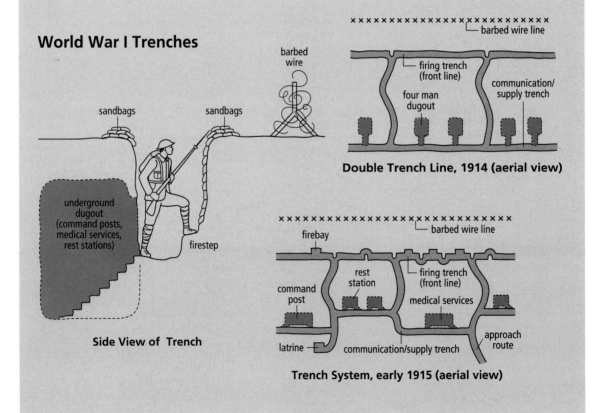

World War I Trenches

Side View of Trench

Double Trench Line, 1914 (aerial view)

Trench System, early 1915 (aerial view)

FAST FACT

TONS OF TONS

During the war, the United States shipped about 7.5 million tons of supplies to France to support the Allied effort. That included 70,000 horses or mules, as well as almost 50,000 trucks, 27,000 freight cars, and 1,800 locomotives.

The worst act of sabotage occurred on July 30, 1916, when a mountain of munitions being shipped to the Allies blew up in New York Harbor. The site was called Black Tom Island, a huge loading dock for ships going to Europe. More than two million pounds of ammunition and explosives were destroyed, as well as Black Tom Island itself. Molten metal tore holes in the Statue of Liberty, and windows blew out throughout the city. Because it was Sunday, few people were killed or hurt. In 1939 an international commission ruled that Germany was responsible for the sabotage.

The Black Tom Island explosion cost the Allies much needed supplies. Many of these supplies would have gone to help fight the Battle of the Somme, an area fortified by the Germans along the Somme River in northern France. French and British troops had attacked there on July 1 in an effort to draw German manpower and arms away from the fighting at Verdun. This battle lasted five months and cost the lives of about 415,000 men. In August Romania entered the war on the side of the Allies and attacked Austria-Hungary. But this had little effect on the fighting at Verdun or along the Somme River.

More men were killed at the Battle of the Somme than the United States had in all of its armed forces and the National Guard combined. In the summer of 1916, Congress requested government money to build new battleships and passed the National Defense Act to increase the armed forces. But the battles Americans were gearing up for in the summer of 1916 were the November presidential and congressional elections.

French infantrymen (land troops) engage in heavy fighting on the Somme. This battle was the bloodiest of the entire war.

ARMAMENTS IN WORLD WAR I

World War I introduced the widespread use of the machine gun—a weapon Hiram Maxim patented in the United States in 1884. The Maxim, as it was called, weighed about 100 pounds and was water cooled. Long belts of bullets entered the gun one by one, and it could be fired at the rate of 450 to 600 rounds per minute.

Most machine guns used in World War I were based on the Maxim design. They included the German Maschinengewehr 08, the British Vickers, and the U.S. Army's 0.30 caliber Browning machine gun. Surrounded by barbed wire (invented in the United States in 1873), these heavy machine guns were used most effectively as defensive weapons. Machine gunners in trenches would hold their position by shooting enemy soldiers going "over the top" of their trenches to attack them.

Machine gun technology was new in World War I. This U.S. soldier is aiming a Lewis gun.

Lighter machine guns, including America's Marlin 0.30, the German Maschinengewehr 08/15, and a modified British Vickers, were attached to airplanes. When the war began, airplanes were mainly used to observe military actions. Later, with mounted guns, they were used to shoot down enemy aircraft in dogfights (airplane battles) and to kill troops on the ground.

Rifles continued to be an important offensive weapon in World War I. The most common ones—German Mauser, British Lee-Enfield, French Lebel, and American Springfield—were somewhat similar. The Mauser's superior design made it accurate, dependable, and quick to reload. Its main drawback was that it used a five-cartridge magazine (supply chamber from which cartridges are fed into the rifle), while Allied rifles could handle slightly larger magazines.

The Ford Motor Company produced this two-man tank just before the end of the war.

Another new weapon in World War I was the British-designed land ship, which moved across terrain on moving tracks. Invented by future British prime minister Winston Churchill, its code name was "tank." The first British tank—called Little Willie—surprised the German army (which hadn't yet developed tanks) in December 1915. Little Willie weighed about four tons, traveled about three miles an hour, and carried three men in its hot, fume-filled interior. The early British tanks became stuck in mud and could not cross trenches. But tanks could rumble through barbed wire and withstand enemy fire. Several months later, the British developed a more reliable series of tanks.

Germany eventually built a few tanks. On April 24, 1918, the first tank-to-tank warfare took place, with the tanks firing machine guns and larger six pounder guns. The British tanks won. By the time the war ended, the Allies had produced more than 6,500 tanks. Germany, which failed to see the importance of tanks, produced 20.

Mortars were used well before World War I, but improved designs made mortars more effective. A mortar is basically a tube that shoots some sort of ammunition almost straight up into the air so that it comes down directly on the enemy. Mortars were well suited to trench warfare. The largest German mortar was called a *minenwerfer* or "mine thrower." It had a 10-inch barrel and lobbed a giant shell filled with metal balls that scattered in the explosion of the shell to inflict wounds on everyone nearby.

By early 1915, the British perfected the Stokes mortar, which the Allies used widely. It was a simpler design than the German mortars, but effective. A bomb about 3 inches in diameter was dropped into a tube. An explosive cartridge at the bottom of the bomb hit a firing pin at the base of the mortar, hurling the bomb from the tube. The Stokes mortar could fire as many as 22 bombs a minute, with each bomb loaded by hand, and hit targets 1,200 yards away.

The French had what German soldiers called the Devil Gun. At 75-mm, this cannon was slightly smaller than the Stokes mortar in diameter but had a longer barrel. It was accurate up to 4 miles. The French military commanders claimed that its Devil Gun won the war.

An Allied rail gun fires its huge shell at the enemy.

TURNING POINTS

During the 1916 election campaigns, Woodrow Wilson ran against Supreme Court Justice Charles Evans Hughes. Hughes and fellow Republicans criticized Wilson for refusing to launch a full-scale invasion of Mexico. Democrats rallied around Wilson with the slogan "He kept us out of war." But the war they meant was the one in Europe. Jane Addams, a strong supporter of peace, came out in favor of Wilson's reelection. Addams approved of Wilson's positions on woman suffrage (the right to vote), child welfare, and better conditions for workers. The presidential election was a close race. On November 7, Woodrow Wilson won only 49 percent of the vote, but that was enough to beat Hughes.

At about the same time as the elections in the United States, the Allies finally fought their way from Greece into Serbia, the tiny country whose struggle to free Bosnia-Herzegovina snowballed into the Great War. The Allies entered into secret

Hi There!

In October 1916, a U-53 (a large German submarine) surfaced in the harbor of Newport, Rhode Island. The captain went ashore to buy newspapers, deliver a letter to the German ambassador, and to impress Americans with the power of the German navy.

treaties to carve up the lands they planned to win from the Central Powers. But the war was far from over.

With the elections behind him, Woodrow Wilson once again pushed for peace, this time using the United States' economic clout. The Allies depended heavily on the United States for supplies but had little money to pay for them. Wilson worked to make it hard for American banks to lend to foreign companies. He hoped that Britain and France would then be willing to listen to plans for peace.

But just when Wilson got ready to issue his peace proposal, Germany proposed a conference to end the war. Britain and France rejected Germany's offer. They were determined to have an all-out victory on the battlefield, even though Germany then occupied all of Belgium and part of France.

Wilson was not about to give up. He sent his proposal to Germany and the Allies a few days later. He urged them to consider "the formation of a league of nations to ensure peace and justice throughout the world." But none of these nations, including Germany, was at that point ready to pursue peace.

On January 22, 1917, Wilson took his case for peace to the U.S. Senate. He urged the nations in Europe to stop fighting a war of attrition. Wilson proposed a "community of power" that would arise from a "peace without victory." He stated that only "a peace among equals can last." Senator La Follette and many others applauded Wilson's speech. La Follette later remarked: "We have just passed through a very important hour in the life of the world."

Although the American people might have been listening, European leaders were not. The Allies refused to negotiate a settlement. As Wilson soon found out, Germany had already taken two actions that would bring the United States even closer to joining the war.

TWO STEPS TOO FAR

On January 9, 1917, German military leaders decided to resume submarine warfare without any restrictions. The Germans had more than 100 larger and stronger U-boats, enough to seriously harm Atlantic shipping. Ten days after this U-boat decision, the German foreign secretary, Arthur Zimmermann, sent a secret cable to the German ambassador in Mexico. The cable announced the start-up of submarine warfare. It also offered an alliance with Mexico if the United States declared war on Germany. In exchange for Mexico's help, Germany would help Mexico win back Arizona, New Mexico, and Texas, which Mexico had lost to the United States in the Mexican-American War (1846–1848).

On January 31, Count Johann von Bernstorff, the German ambassador to the United States, called on Secretary of State Robert Lansing. He informed Lansing that the pledge Germany made after sinking the *Sussex* was canceled. Germany planned to start submarine warfare the next day. On February 3, the United States formally broke diplomatic relations with Germany. Count von Bernstorff was asked to leave, and the American ambassador in Germany came home.

President Wilson announces to Congress the official break in diplomatic relations with Germany.

British spies got hold of the Zimmermann telegram to Mexico and released the information to U.S. officials. When President Wilson broke the news, many Americans demonstrated their desire for war. They staged parades and carried signs reading "Let's Get the Hun," an insulting name for a German soldier.

Ernest Hemingway

An estimated 15,000 Americans had already joined the Allied fight in Europe. Among these were novelists Ernest Hemingway, who drove an ambulance in Italy, and William Faulkner, who joined the Royal Canadian Air Force.

Some of the Americans were part of medical units. One group formed its own unit, or escadrille, in the French Air Service. Others fought with the French or British armies. While visiting their aunt's house in Britain, Harold and Howard Hudson noticed a military training camp next door. These 15-year-old twins from Bridgeport, Connecticut, gave their ages as 19 and signed up with the British army.

March 4, 1917, was the date set for the newly reelected president to take office and start leading the nation. On that day, Woodrow Wilson went to a room in the Capitol Building to sign a few bills. At noon he got up from his chair, took the presidential oath of office, then sat down again to continue his work. The *New York Times* described it as the "strangest inauguration in history."

The transition from one government to the next in Russia was much more dramatic. Russia had an agreement with Britain and France to attack Germany if Germany attacked either country. Russia lived up to the agreement but at a tremendous cost. By the end of 1916, the Russians fought their last offensive against the Germans in the mountains of Eastern Europe. Russian troops ran out of supplies. More than one million Russian soldiers died. The Russian government was in chaos. The Russian people were sick of war.

In March 1917, Russian workers went on strike. The Russian Duma, or parliament, forced Czar Nicholas II from power and organized a temporary government. Russia seemed headed for democracy. When word reached Washington, Edith Wilson wrote in her diary: "Thrilling news from Russia. . . . Overthrow of the Government and taking control by the people."

Meanwhile, more Americans seemed ready to enter the Great War. Donald Ryerson, a Chicago businessman, thought war was inevitable. Ryerson enlisted in the U.S. Navy. While waiting for his orders, he organized a group of speakers called the Four-Minute Men.

The United States in 1917 was home to many immigrants. Many of them, as well as many native English speakers, could not read English. Ryerson's men found a clever way to inform and persuade these people about the war. Each day, about 10 to 13 million people went to the movies. The movies

Czar Nicholas II poses with three of his daughters in a Russian forest. The czar and his entire family were later assassinated on the orders of Russia's new Communist government.

FAST FACT

TALK, TALK, TALK
During U.S. involvement in World War I, more than 75,000 people gave about 7.5 million four-minute pro-war speeches in movie theaters and elsewhere to about 314.5 million people.

were on film wound around two or more reels. It took four minutes to change from one movie reel to another. The Four-Minute Men used this time to speak to their audience about the war.

WAR

Ryerson gave the first four-minute speech at Chicago's Strand Theater on April 1 or 2. President Wilson called Congress into special session on April 2. It took Congress

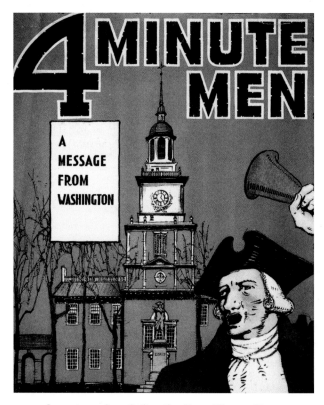

A poster advertisting the Four-Minute Men

nearly all day to gather in the chamber of the House of Representatives (House), along with members of the Supreme Court, foreign ambassadors, and other dignitaries. That evening, Wilson told them that the United States would fight to "make the world safe for democracy." He asked Congress to "declare the recent course of the Imperial German Government to be in fact nothing less than war against the government and people of the United States."

The wild applause that followed shocked Wilson deeply. After returning to the White House, he said to Joseph Tumulty, his secretary, "My message today was a message of death for our young men. How strange it seems to applaud that." Then the president of the United States broke down and cried.

On April 4, the Senate voted yes on the war resolution. Two days later, the House did the same. Not everyone voted for war—6 senators and 50 representatives voted against the resolution. Among them were Jeanette Rankin from Montana, the first woman elected to Congress, and Senator La Follette.

Frances Witherspoon and Tracy Mygatt were witnesses to the House vote, which was taken behind closed doors. The two women had come to Washington to join some 5,000 people in the Mass Meeting for Peace held on April 2 at the Capitol. They and several others hid in the House visitor's gallery and listened to the vote on the night of April 6, 1917. Since this was Good Friday, the day that Jesus was betrayed in the Christian Bible, the two young women described the vote as "a particularly solemn night of betrayal."

President Wilson signed the resolution into law that very night. As soon as he finished signing, an aide to the secretary of the navy signaled to an officer in the navy department not far from the White House. Soon a message was relayed to American ships at sea: WAR.

One of the first official actions of the Wilson administration after the declaration of war was to establish the Committee on Public Information (CPI). According to the order establishing the agency, the purpose of the CPI was to portray the "absolute justice of America's cause." George Creel, editor of the *Rocky Mountain News*, was the head of the agency. The war was in Europe, and private citizens in the United States did not have radios that could receive messages from across the vast Atlantic Ocean. For this reason, Creel controlled almost all the information that came into the country from European battlefields.

Creel also created and paid for much of the pro-war propaganda (printed information used to spread ideas) manufactured in the United States. With the help of the CPI, the Four-Minute Men program, which started in Chicago, spread rapidly across the nation.

In May Wilson appointed General John Pershing to lead the American Expeditionary Force (AEF) in Europe. Pershing stopped chasing Pancho Villa in Mexico and returned home. It was time to prepare an American armed force to fight in Europe.

Pershing went to see what was happening in Europe for himself. Dodging German submarines, his ship made it to Liverpool, England, on June 8. In ceremony after ceremony, Pershing was welcomed as the savior of the Allied cause.

By the time Pershing arrived in France, Paris was dangerously open to enemy

A poster created by the Committee on Public Information urges Americans to conserve food.

invasion. French soldiers had been ordered to fight off the Germans in the Champagne region of France, but their attack failed miserably. Many French soldiers, outnumbered and overwhelmed after three years of war, threw down their rifles and refused to fight.

William Sharp, the U.S. ambassador to France, held a dinner party in Paris to honor Pershing. At the party, the ambassador put into words what others might have been thinking: "You cannot realize the satisfaction I feel that we are in the war and that you are here to prepare for our participation. . . . I hope you have not arrived too late."

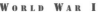
THE ENEMY'S POINT OF VIEW IN WORLD WAR I

By 1900 European countries could expand on their continent only by moving into territory claimed by a neighboring country. Most European nations also competed fiercely for influence and trading centers in Asia and Africa.

Germany, like its neighbors, wanted the wealth and power that foreign colonies and more land in Europe would bring. Tensions increased as smaller regions, such as Serbia, wanted to gain or maintain their independence. Germany, Russia, Britain, and France were involved in diplomatic schemes and armed conflicts in Siberia, the Balkans (countries in a peninsula along the southeastern part of Europe), and elsewhere in the years before World War I. Alliances among the countries kept shifting in reaction to relatively short, local wars.

Curious crowds fill the streets of Berlin in cars and on foot to hear the German government formally declare war on Serbia in 1914. Germany and its allies expected to win the war quickly and easily. Many German people were confident and unconcerned early on.

When war broke out in the summer of 1914, Germans, Austrians, and Hungarians thought the armed conflict would be short, as other recent wars had been. Like the Allies, the Germans thought their soldiers would be home by Christmas.

By 1916 the Austrians and Hungarians were tired of the war. But the motto of the German people was *durchhaltern* (see it through). The British blockade of German ports caused hunger, even starvation, throughout Germany. But the German defeat of the Russian and Italian armies brought hope that the war would soon end with Germany's honor intact.

The rise of Communism in Russia was reflected in unrest in Germany too. In the summer of 1917, workers' strikes and several mutinies in the navy took place. The German people began to question the wisdom of their military leaders and the goal of victory at all costs. Political parties, which had stood united in the first part of the war, began to take differing positions on whether to continue the conflict.

When German military leaders decided in late 1918 that the war could not be won, they encouraged the kaiser to give up his rule and allow the formation of a republic. Based on a constitution drawn up in Weimar, a German city, the new republic was led mostly by the Social Democratic Party. But the party did not enact many social or democratic reforms in its early years. The average German did not lead a better life economically. During negotiations for the treaty that officially ended World War I, military and political leaders within the Weimar Republic tried to keep the military strong within Germany, in case of uprising by the Communists or other groups. The harsh terms of the treaty made it difficult for the Weimar Republic to survive. The weakened German economy and military made it easier for Adolf Hitler and the Nazi Party to eventually come to power after the war.

OVER THERE

4

In the spring of 1917, only about 200,000 men were in the U.S. National Guard (trained personnel who could be called up to serve in emergencies) and the regular army (full-time, professional soldiers). In the months leading up to the United States' declaration of war and shortly afterward, another 300,000 men volunteered to serve. But 500,000 soldiers was far from enough.

Congress passed the Selective Service Act, which created a new national army. All American men between the ages of 21 and 30 were required to register for the draft. On June 5, between 7 A.M. and 7 P.M., these men were to go to a local selective service board and have their names placed on "the lists of honor."

There were 4,500 selective service boards across the nation, some with as many as 10,500 men of draft age in their area. As bands played and Boy Scouts helped the draftees line up, everyone who registered got a number from 1 to 10,500. For 17 hours straight, blindfolded men picked numbers from a glass bowl.

Newton Baker, the secretary of war, selected the first number: 258. All draftees with number 258 were the first ones called by their draft boards. They were examined and declared eligible or exempt. The boards gave exemptions (releases from service) to men who were government officials, had war-related jobs, had family relying on them for financial support, or had health problems.

The Draft

The U.S. government has the power to require—or draft—citizens to join the armed forces in defense of the nation. A military draft is also called conscription and had been used in the United States since the Revolutionary War. In 1973, after the unpopular Vietnam War, the United States stopped drafting men into military service. But later, it required certain citizens to register with the government so they can be drafted if there is a national emergency.

During World War I, draft numbers were pulled from a glass container by a blindfolded man.

All these new soldiers needed officers. The War Department set up officer training camps across the country. Charles Whittlesey, who led the Lost Battalion, was one of the first new officers. The U.S. armed forces were segregated. So the War Department set up a separate school at Fort Des Moines, Iowa, to train African Americans for leadership positions in the military.

African American men sign up for Negro Officers Training Camp at Fort Des Moines in Iowa.

The war effort meant high-paying jobs for thousands of workers, particularly in manufacturing armaments and explosives. Some of the arms were of American design, but many were simply the ones used in Europe at the time. By the spring of 1917, American workers were producing more than 15,000 British and Russian rifles each day.

The Allies also needed food and other supplies. President Wilson and Congress set up the U.S. Food Administration, headed by future president Herbert Hoover, and the U.S. Fuel Administration, headed by Harry Garfield. The Food Administration issued registration cards for housewives (most women did not work outside the home then) across the country. The person signing the card pledged "to carry out the directions and advice of the Food Administrator in the conduct of my household as my circumstances permit."

First Lady Edith Wilson was the first woman to sign a registration card and send

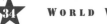

it to the Food Administration's office. Mrs. Wilson and wives of other U.S. officials also sewed garments for the war effort. Mrs. Wilson borrowed a flock of 14 sheep and 4 lambs to graze at the White House. When the sheep were sheared, their wool was sold at special auctions. The money went to the Red Cross, which provided medical care to soldiers and civilians in war-torn countries.

Meanwhile, Americans scrimped and saved to send food to Europe. The government set up wheatless days and meatless days. The U.S. Food Administration put slogans on everything from theater curtains to gum wrappers. One slogan for meatless days read "Don't let your horse be more patriotic than you are—eat a dish of oatmeal." Another slogan read "If U fast U beat U boats—if U feast U boats beat U."

Because of this food management, thousands of tons of food went to U.S. and Allied forces in Europe during the war. The United States eventually shipped overseas almost 10 billion pounds of dairy products, meat, fats, and vegetable oils, as well as more than one billion bushels of grain and other cereal products.

Americans also bought Liberty Bonds, which were basically IOUs from the U.S. government in exchange for cash. The first campaign for these bonds started in June 1917. John Philip Sousa composed the "Liberty Bond March." Money from these bonds went to help not only the United States, but also Britain and other Allies. By the time the United States entered the war, Britain had used up all its gold and other credit. The Allied war

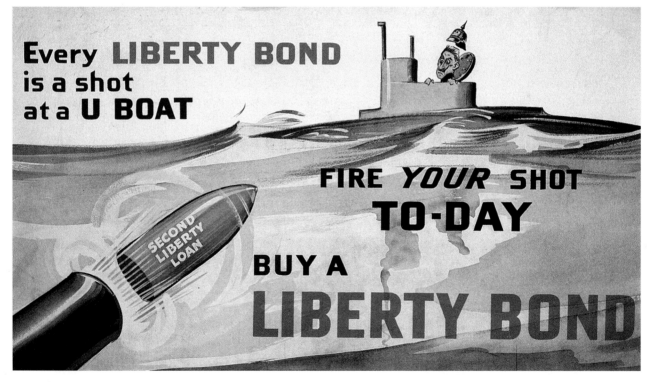

The Committee on Public Information created and distributed many posters encouraging Americans to buy Liberty Bonds as a show of support for U.S. troops in Europe.

effort depended on billions of dollars from the U.S. Treasury.

"THE YANKS ARE COMING"

In 1917 George M. Cohan wrote "Over There." The song was so patriotic that Congress later awarded him a special medal for it. The lyrics told the Allies that "the Yanks [Americans] are coming . . . and they won't come back 'til it's over over there [in Europe]."

By the end of June, the first Yanks—also called doughboys—reached France. Wilson had made Pershing commander in chief of U.S. forces. French and British military officers, however, wanted the U.S. soldiers to be divided among the Allied Forces. Pershing demanded that the American Expeditionary Force (AEF) remain a separate fighting unit. While the generals figured out how these men would be deployed (put to work), the troops trained with the French army.

The Allies did not want German spy planes to discover where the Americans were. So many of the troops stayed in barns in the French countryside. Like the

American doughboys

French soldiers, the doughboys were shuttled from place to place by train. The officers sat in passenger cars, but the regular soldiers traveled in "forty and eight"—boxcars that could fit either 40 men or 8 horses.

The 1st and 2nd Divisions of the American Expeditionary Force were training in Europe by September. Pershing set up U.S. military headquarters at Chaumont, France, along a main railroad line. The railroad system was vitally important in bringing supplies to the battlefront. Pershing persuaded the French to give him control over the railroad lines in exchange for American-built locomotives whose wheels were made to fit French tracks.

Another priority for Pershing was the telephone system. The U.S. Army Signal Corps installed new lines and paid for

FAST FACT

DOUGHBOYS

It's not clear where the term "doughboys" came from, but it was used before World War I. During the Mexican War of 1846–1848, infantrymen were often covered with the white dust of adobe soils. "Adobies" might have become "dobies" and then "doughboys." In the Civil War (1861–1865), mounted soldiers called infantrymen "doughboys," perhaps because these soldiers used flour or white clay to polish their white belts.

Hello Girls

General Pershing called them switchboard soldiers, but many American soldiers called them Hello Girls. These American women served as telephone operators for Pershing's forces in Europe. The women were fluent in French and English and were specially trained by the American Telephone and Telegraph Company. During World War I, they were not considered part of the military, but in 1979 the U.S. Army finally gave war medals and veterans benefits to the few Hello Girls who were still alive.

other lines from the French. The War Department sent over about 100 U.S. operators who were fluent in French.

On September 5, 1917, a German artillery shell exploded near Cambrai, France, injuring two Americans working on the railroad lines. Although these men were members of an engineering unit, not a combat unit, they were still America's first official military casualties of the Great War.

The U.S. troops received a few months of training in trench warfare, and most were first sent to relatively quiet areas along the Western Front. The 26th Division (National Guardsmen) arrived in September and spent months manning communication lines. The 42nd Division (National Guardsmen), led by Douglas MacArthur, landed in October and later joined French troops in a relatively safe area in the Vosges Mountains of eastern

France. The 42nd was also called the Rainbow Division because it had National Guardsmen from every state in the Union.

The 1st Division, nicknamed the Big Red One, was regular army and soon saw real combat. October 23, 1917, marked the first shot from an American-manned gun and the first wounding of a U.S. soldier in combat. The first combat deaths of Americans happened near Verdun, France, on the night of November 2.

In the same few weeks that the United States was beginning to play an active part in the war, Russia stopped fighting completely. Russia's new Bolshevik (Communist)

FAST FACT

Bolsheviks were members of the Russian Communist Party who supported the leadership of Vladimir Lenin. Lenin called his followers "bolsheviks," which comes from a Russian word for "majority."

regime began negotiating with Germany for a separate peace treaty.

While the Allies tried to keep Russia in the war, the Italians lost an important battle against Germany and Austria-Hungary near Kobarid, in Austria-Hungary. The German army was then able to shift many divisions from Italy to the war on the Western Front.

Faced with an increased threat by the German army along the Western Front, the Allied generals and chiefs of staff met in Paris. They came up with a more unified plan for fighting. The Americans would be responsible for some sectors of the battle-front and would coordinate maneuvers with British and French troops, under French field marshal Ferdinand Foch. Though still not well prepared for battle, the Americans boosted the morale of the Allies' war-weary troops.

BATTLING THE COLD

The end of 1917 brought unusually cold weather. Added to the constant barrage of artillery, the mud and vermin in the trenches, and the closeness of maiming and death, the doughboys also suffered miserably from the frigid conditions. So did most of the soldiers fighting in Europe then. The supply system in France was still unable to gather and transport the enormous amount of equipment needed at the front. The doughboys didn't have enough winter clothing or blankets. Some marched in the snow with rags on their feet. The lucky ones who had boots found their toes frozen to the leather.

The harsh winter, plus crowding at army camps, brought death to the soldiers training in the United States as well. At Camp Funston in Kansas, measles, pneumonia, meningitis, and influenza killed about three men a day.

Coal was a source of heat and power for Americans. In late 1917 U.S. homeowners struggled to heat their homes because factories making war supplies need the coal to power their machinery. The U.S. Fuel Administration shut down factories making non-military goods to make more coal available to U.S. citizens.

U.S. soldiers take aim from snow-covered trenches in December 1917.

UNIFORMS IN WORLD WAR I

American doughboys wore steel helmets in battle.

U.S. troops

The U.S. soldier in full battle dress carried a backpack weighing as much as 70 pounds. This included his weapon and ammunition, gas mask, blanket roll, canteen, rations, and a small shovel. In battle a doughboy wore a steel helmet with a rim around it that looked like an upside-down bowl. His khaki-colored uniform consisted of a four-pocket tunic with a stand-up collar and breeches or trousers. Doughboys had leather boots or high-top shoes and leggings (puttees) of white fabric that wrapped around their calves.

U.S. officers wore heavy gabardine trench coats for cold weather, and regular troops were issued raincoats made from waterproof canvas. As Americans spent more time in the trenches, they started to wear the leather and fur sleeveless vest (jerkin) that was a favorite of the British army. The jerkin came down to the soldier's hips or midthigh. It kept his body warm but let his arms move freely. Yanks in the trenches wore rubber wading boots in an effort to keep their feet dry. These boots trapped moisture inside them and caused as many foot problems as they were intended to cure.

A German soldier crouches with his rifle.

An American officer

German troops

German soldiers also carried a heavy backpack, containing similar equipment. Early in the war, the German soldiers had a close-fitting steel helmet with a spike on top. (The style later changed.) The standard German uniform was gray, with a turned-down collar and more decoration than most U.S. uniforms. German soldiers had leather overcoats, stiff leather backpacks, and high leather boots.

Doughboy Slang

cooties: body lice, fleas, and bedbugs. Also called "seam squirrels" and "pants rabbits."

dogfight: aerial combat

go over the top: to leave the relative safety of a trench and charge the enemy across no-man's-land

monkey meat: foul-tasting canned ration of beef and carrots

no-man's-land: the area between the trenches of warring troops

whizzbang: a shell from heavy artillery, particularly the Austrian 88-mm gun

By 1917 the continued blockade of supplies into Germany had driven the death rate among German civilians to an average of 700 a day. That winter the extreme cold would make the death toll climb even higher.

German general Erich Ludendorff met his other advisers to decide on their next step. Germany was running out of supplies and manpower, just like the Allies. If Germany was to win the war, the German army had to go on the offensive before more American troops arrived in Europe to overwhelm the Germans. Ludendorff knew that his only chance was to strike in the spring of 1918. He hoped that German U-boats could slow the flow of doughboys coming to Europe.

FOURTEEN POINTS

On January 8, 1918, as Germany shifted more troops to the Western Front, President Wilson proposed a fourteen-point plan for peace. Addressing Congress that day, he stated: "We demand that the world be made fit and safe to live in." Wilson set forth his plans for a league of nations that would help settle international disputes. He called for equality in international trade, the end of secret treaties, and freedom of the seas in both peace and war.

Many of Wilson's points were similar to proposals from the International Congress of Women that had met in the Netherlands in 1915. The European powers had not listened then, but a lot had happened since. French and British soldiers had suffered greatly in the trenches of France and Belgium, with few victories to show for it. During the summer and fall of 1917, for example, nearly 245,000 Allied soldiers on the Western Front were killed or wounded. They had captured only about 9,000 yards of ground. Since the war began, battle lines in France and Belgium had moved no more than about 10 miles in any direction. Italy was nearly exhausted. Many French soldiers had mutinied. Britain was heavily in debt.

Wilson hoped that with this stalemate, costly in money and human lives, the Fourteen Points would have a better chance. But Britain, France, and Germany were not ready for peace. The Allies had secret plans to divide any conquered territories based on Germany's complete surrender. And Germany still planned to win. Mocking Wilson's view of international relations, the French premier Georges Clemenceau compared Wilson's Fourteen Points to Biblical commandments. "God," he said, "only needed ten."

OVER THE TOP

So the war went on. The Allies needed more men. Although the U.S. draft boards had filled their quota (required number of soldiers), in August 1917, Congress changed the draft law to make all men between 18 and 45 eligible for the draft.

As troops in the trenches shivered through February and the first part of March 1918, something odd happened along the northern coast of Spain. People got sick for about three days, then recovered. What was unusual about the disease was that most of the people who got it were young, healthy adults. This illness was soon called Spanish influenza.

On March 3, Germany and Russia formally signed the Brest-Litovsk Treaty. This treaty ended hostilities between the two nations on terms very favorable to Germany. About a week later, Newton Baker, the United States secretary of war, sailed into the harbor at Brest, France. He came to tour the front lines with General Pershing.

More U.S. troops arrived around that time as well. The 32nd and 41st Divisions joined the four divisions (1st, 2nd, 26th, and 42nd) that had spent the winter in France. Soldiers in a U.S. cavalry (mounted) unit that arrived in March showed signs of Spanish influenza. The same odd disease hit back in the United States too. The first place it was reported was among the 20,000 soldiers training at Camp Funston, in Kansas.

Within a few weeks, other army camps reported cases of the flu.

GERMANY'S FINAL PUSH

Meanwhile, an attack of a different sort was in the making. German general Erich Ludendorff planned five major offensives along the Western Front that he hoped would win the war for Germany. The first was scheduled for March 21, along the Somme River, in an area between Arras and St. Quentin, France, held jointly by British and French forces.

The first barrage of German artillery began at dawn on March 21, along a 40-mile stretch of trenches near Cambrai. The odds were heavily in Germany's favor, with 69 German divisions facing 33 British divisions. The German army also had about twice as many heavy guns as the British. The next day, a huge German gun with a 75-mile range opened fire. It was able to shoot artillery shells into Paris.

British and French political leaders, including French president Raymond Poincaré, met to map out their strategy and establish a unified military command. They decided that French field marshal Ferdinand Foch would be in charge of the Allied defense.

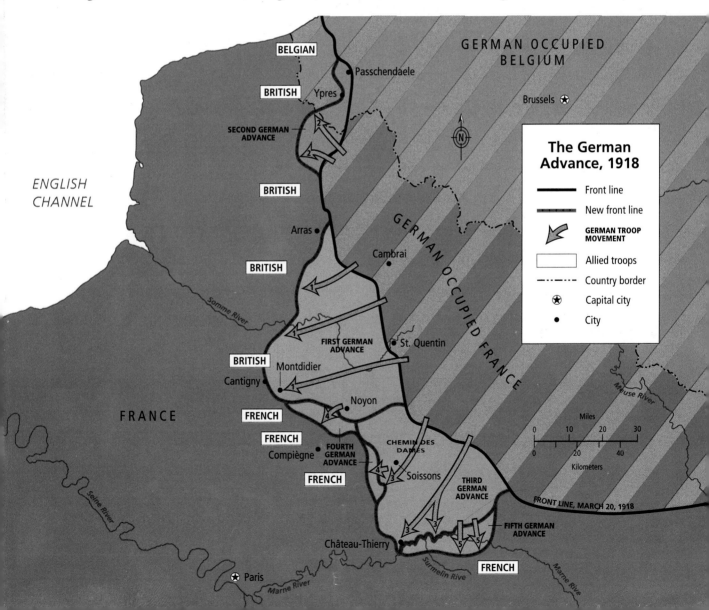

General Pershing was not invited to the meeting, probably because he was meeting with Secretary of War Baker. The French and British also were sure that President Wilson would agree to put U.S. forces under Foch's command. On March 28, two days after the meeting, Pershing visited Foch and, in his halting French, agreed to the plan.

By April hundreds of thousands of doughboys were in France. About 250,000 more were scheduled to come every month after that. The United States organized its first air force in April as well. Although Foch would have wished for more men, the force was the best Pershing could muster.

EYEWITNESS QUOTE

"Infantry, artillery, aviation, all that we have is yours; use them as you wish. More will come, in numbers equal to the requirements."

—U.S. general Pershing to French field marshal Foch, 1918

The British did most of the fighting during the second German offensive in early April. At the end of April, doughboys saw their first fighting against the German army. The date was April 20, 1918. The place, a small French town called Seicheprey, was in an area called the St. Mihiel Salient.

A salient bulging out into enemy lines is hard to defend. The French had created this bulge in 1914 and wanted to smooth it out by capturing surrounding territory. The American 1st Division—the Big Red One—took up a position there in January, relieving the French 1st Moroccan Division. In March the Americans, led by

Three brave doughboys go over the top at the charge on the St. Mihiel Salient.

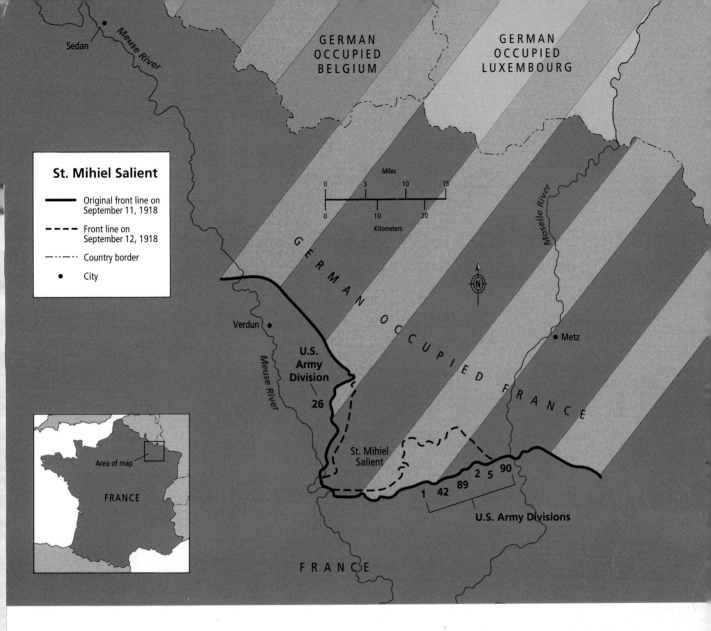

St. Mihiel Salient

— Original front line on
September 11, 1918

- - - Front line on
September 12, 1918

—·—·— Country border

• City

GERMAN
OCCUPIED
BELGIUM

GERMAN
OCCUPIED
LUXEMBOURG

Sedan

Meuse River

Miles

0   5   10   15

0   10   20

Kilometers

G E R M A N   O C C U P I E D   F R A N C E

Moselle River

Verdun

N

Metz

U.S.
Army
Division

26

Meuse River

St. Mihiel
Salient

2 5 90

1   42   89

U.S. Army Divisions

Area of map

FRANCE

F R A N C E

division commander Robert Bullard, staged several raids on the German lines. The Germans were preparing a counterattack to teach the Americans a lesson when the Big Red One left to fight in another sector. The 26th Division, commanded by Clarence Edwards, took its place.

The German raid on April 20 pitted about 3,000 German troops against about 600 relatively inexperienced New England Yankees. French troops in the area tried to help, but the Germans took 136 American prisoners and inflicted heavy casualties. The next day, the Americans counterattacked and the Germans withdrew.

Both Germany and the United States claimed victory. Back in the United States, Creel's Committee on Public Information released its most famous propaganda movie, *The Kaiser, the Beast of Berlin*. The U.S. public read stories of German atrocities, some of which were true and some not.

FAST FACT

WATCH YOUR LANGUAGE

During World War I, American hamburgers (named after the German city of Hamburg) were instead called "Salisbury steak," frankfurters (named for Frankfurt, Germany) became "liberty sausages," and dachshunds became "liberty dogs." Schools stopped teaching German, and German-language books were burned.

Even if Americans did not believe Creel's propaganda, Congress made it difficult to speak out against the war with the Sedition Act, which President Wilson signed into law on May 16. Americans could be fined $10,000 or sent to prison for 20 years for showing disloyalty to the United States. Government agencies and citizens groups investigated the loyalty of thousands of Americans and harassed many innocent citizens at home. Yet U.S. soldiers fought overseas for democratic principles, such as the right to free speech.

Throughout the spring, more of the Allied troops suffered from the Spanish flu. German troops probably had the same ailment. General Ludendorff called it Flanders fever. The men were sick with a high fever for a few days. Almost all recovered.

Pershing planned to attack the Germans at the end of May. The Big Red One moved into position for a battle at Cantigny, France. On May 27, the day before the planned attack, General Ludendorff launched his third major offensive. This one was aimed southward from Chemin des Dames toward the Marne River. French forces had to move to protect Paris. But

Pershing decided to stick by his plan and attack the Germans at Cantigny anyway.

On May 28, the Americans took Cantigny. Because there was no French artillery to stop them, the German forces shelled the town heavily. But the doughboys refused to give up. Military commanders later admitted that territory gained was not worth the lives lost.

Ludendorff's attack was originally supposed to draw French troops away from battlefields such as Cantigny. As French troops retreated, this offensive turned out to be more successful than expected. Ludendorff decided to push the German army forward, toward Paris, hoping that France would ask for peace if the French capital was threatened.

At France's request, Pershing brought the 2nd Division to help defend against the German advance, since the Big Red One was too far away. Traveling along the Paris-Metz Highway, doughboys met retreating French soldiers who declared that the war was over. And it might have been if the German army had a better supply line.

Meanwhile, the 2nd Division, led by Major General Omar Bundy, stopped about 40 miles outside of Paris and dug in. They stayed in foxholes (hastily dug pits) for three days while French soldiers tried and failed to hold back the German army.

Major General Omar Bundy

By June 3, the German army was only 56 miles from Paris.

THE HOME FRONT IN WORLD WAR I

In 1914 most Americans were content to let European nations settle their own disputes. U.S. industry profited from supplying the warring countries, and U.S. workers found plenty of new jobs manufacturing war supplies.

The realities of war "over there" hit closer to home, when the United States entered the war. Americans were urged to send their young men overseas to fight, and thousands of men were drafted into the armed forces. The public endured shortages, as food and fuel were redirected to soldiers and starving civilians in Europe. At the same time, Americans were asked to contribute money to the war effort by buying war bonds.

Americans were flooded with pro-war propaganda. There were patriotic speeches at the movies and posters and pamphlets everywhere. Food Administrator Herbert Hoover urged Americans "to lay your double chin on the altar of

FIGHT! BOYS, FIGHT! WE'RE ALL BACK OF YOU

WORDS AND MUSIC BY
Robt. W. Billings

Published by
ROBT. W. BILLINGS
MILWAUKEE, WIS.

Patriotic songs, like the sheet music shown above, were a huge part of U.S. civilian culture during the war. The U.S. public was encouraged to show support for Allied troops in any and every way.

liberty. . . . If we are selfish or even careless, we are disloyal, we are the enemy at home." In the fever of anti-German feeling, schools stopped teaching German and students burned German textbooks. Anti-war feelings were considered un-American. Citizens who voiced opposition to the war could be fined or put in jail.

As World War I continued, Americans became more concerned about the mass killing and horrors of trench warfare. By November 1918, they had grown weary of the shortages of food and other supplies that had gone to the war effort. American families struggled as the cost of living rose. Adding to the economic problems of 1918, influenza killed or sickened millions of Americans. At war's end, Americans seemed eager to put the Great War behind them and avoid further entanglements overseas, including participation in the League of Nations.

This painting depicts the brutal fighting that took place at Belleau Wood in France. By the end of the battle, the U.S. marine brigade had suffered a casualty rate of 55 percent, with 1,062 men killed and 3,615 wounded.

The next day, General Bundy and the men of the 2nd Division were assigned to defend the area. The French general wanted the Americans to withdraw to a stronger position closer to Paris, but General Bundy refused.

The German army was entrenched in a small area called Belleau Wood, about 3,000 yards long and 1,000 yards wide at its widest point. The highest point in the area was Hill 142. Bundy was determined to take the wood and the hill.

On June 6, a brigade of marines in the 2nd Division attacked Hill 142, even though some of the backup troops were not yet in place. Another of the division's marine brigades tried to capture Belleau Wood itself. The Americans lobbed hand grenades and tried to crawl through the barbed wire defenses, dodging machine-gun fire. An American reporter mistakenly thought the

doughboys had won the battle that day and sent home a glorious report. The *Chicago Daily Tribune* ran a banner headline: U.S. MARINES SMASH HUNS.

The German army was not about to give an inch, however. Neither were the Americans. Both sides fought fiercely. German planes flew over the U.S. troops, pummelling them with machine-gun fire. U.S. artillery lobbed poison gas at the Germans. Marines rushed forward in rows, only to be shot down by machine guns. Explosives ripped apart soldiers on both sides.

Bundy's men were not to be denied victory. Eventually, Hill 142 was theirs. And on June 25, the last of the Germans in the area surrendered. The French renamed that charred plot of mud, blood, and rotting flesh Bois de la Brigade de Marine, or "Marine Brigade Forest." The Germans

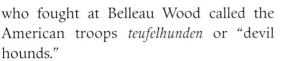

who fought at Belleau Wood called the American troops *teufelhunden* or "devil hounds."

The 2nd Division finished its fighting in that sector by shelling the town of Vaux, which the Americans believed contained German soldiers. By the time the Yanks entered the town, though, it was deserted.

Meanwhile, Ludendorff had opened a fourth offensive on a 20-mile front from Montdidier to Noyon. The German attack began on June 9 but met fierce resistance from French and American forces. By June 14, the German advance was halted.

The month of June proved that the inexperienced U.S. troops could and would fight. But the 2nd Division paid dearly. Of the 17,000 infantrymen who made up the division, about 9,000 had been killed, wounded, or were missing in action.

THE BEGINNING OF THE END

German general Ludendorff decided to try for a fifth time to beat the Allies. Field Marshal Foch, who was in charge of all Allied military strategy, didn't know exactly where and when this next attack would take place. So he didn't know how to place his troops.

Ludendorff launched his fifth offensive along the Marne River in an area held by American, French, and Italian soldiers. The Surmelin River Valley, which was critical to the Allied defense, was under control of the American 3rd Division, led by Major General Joseph Dickman. Dickman's men fought back fiercely.

The 3rd Division troops held their lines, earning them the nickname Rock of the Marne. The French and U.S. forces

Shell Shock

Soldiers trapped in trenches were witnesses to the horrors wrought by the enemy's artillery barrages. Mangled bodies of the dead and dying surrounded them. Soldiers also faced the agony of "going over the top" and fighting the enemy face-to-face in nearby trenches. This caused soldiers to suffer from what the Allies termed "war neurosis" or "shell shock"—posttraumatic stress disorder. It's probable that millions of soldiers had nightmares about digging themselves out of the rubble that had buried them alive or of killing other soldiers at close range. Shell-shocked men had uncontrollable diarrhea, couldn't sleep, stopped speaking, whimpered for hours, or twitched uncontrollably. At least 42,000 U.S. soldiers were discharged due to shell shock. No one knows how many were kept on duty. While some soldiers recovered, others suffered for the rest of their lives.

launched a counteroffensive on July 18, capturing Soissons. One German leader said that the battle of July 15 through 18 was the turning point in the war. "On the 18th even the most optimistic among us knew that all was lost. The history of the world was played out in three days."

In late July 1918, Field Marshal Foch met with the Allied generals—America's John Pershing, Britain's Sir Douglas Haig, and France's Henri-Philippe Pétain—to discuss what to do next. France and Britain could not bring any more men into the battlefield. Four years of war had exhausted the supply of troops and the economies of both countries. But the Americans had more than one million men fighting in Europe and more back in the United States.

EYEWITNESS QUOTE:
THE 3RD DIVISION

"Never have I seen so many dead men, never such frightful battle scenes. . . . The American [soldier] . . . had nerve; we must give him credit for that; but he also displayed a savage roughness. 'The Americans kill everybody!' was the cry of terror of July 15th, which for a long time stuck in the bones of our men."

—German lieutenant Kurt Hesse, 1918

Foch and his generals decided to launch three limited attacks designed to take back railroad lines and put more pressure on the German army. One of them was to free up the Paris-Avricourt railroad line near the St. Mihiel Salient. Foch suggested that the job be done by "the American Army."

Pershing was delighted. This was the first time that the Americans could fight in an army completely under his own, not French, command. Pershing created the American First Army and made himself commanding general. He created several corps, putting General Bullard in charge of IV Corps. General Charles Summerall took Bullard's place leading the Big Red One. The Americans in Europe had an army and a mission of their own. And they had a war to win.

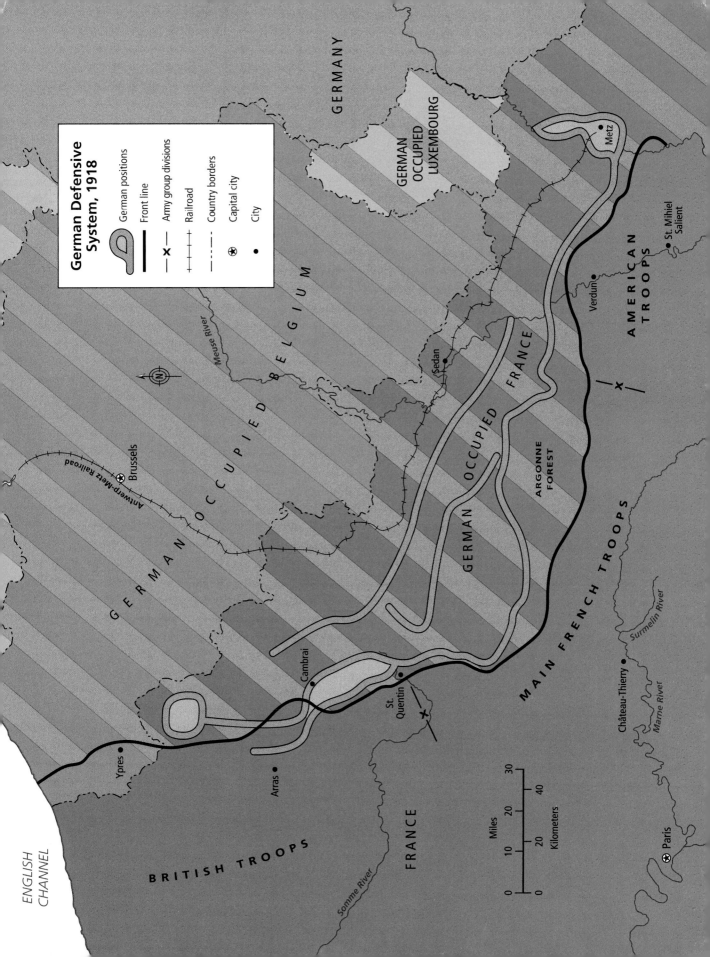

ENGLISH CHANNEL

German Defensive System, 1918

German positions
Front line
X — Army group divisions
⊦⊦⊦ Railroad
Country borders
⊛ Capital city
• City

GERMANY

GERMAN OCCUPIED LUXEMBOURG

Metz

St. Mihiel Salient

Verdun

AMERICAN TROOPS

Meuse River

BELGIUM

GERMAN OCCUPIED

Sedan

GERMAN OCCUPIED FRANCE

ARGONNE FOREST

Brussels

Antwerp-Metz Railroad

MAIN FRENCH TROOPS

Surmelin River

Cambrai

St. Quentin

Château-Thierry

Marne River

BRITISH TROOPS

Ypres

Arras

FRANCE

Somme River

Paris

Miles
30
20
10
0

Kilometers
40
20
0

MEDICAL CARE IN WORLD WAR I

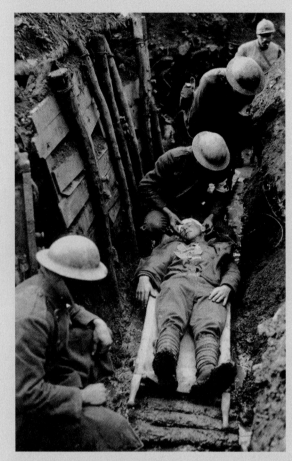

A U.S. marine receives first aid before being sent to a hospital at the rear of the trenches in Toulon, France.

During 1917 and 1918, more U.S. soldiers died from disease, particularly the flu and pneumonia, than from battle. But this statistic includes soldiers stationed in the United States during the war. For U.S. forces serving in Europe, World War I was the first war in which a U.S. soldier engaged in battle was more likely to be killed than to die of disease.

Part of the reason for this change was weapons. Machine guns could kill more soldiers than rifles, for example. But another reason was the drop in death from disease—even with the flu epidemic—due to improvements in medical care.

In World War I, every U.S. soldier was required to get a vaccination against typhoid fever. This greatly reduced the number of deaths from typhoid, which had plagued American soldiers in the Spanish-American War of 1898.

The germ theory of disease was also clearly accepted by the time World War I began. As a result, camp facilities and drinking water were kept as clean as possible, although the conditions in the trenches were sometimes horrible. Antibiotics, such as penicillin, had not yet been discovered, but antiseptics, such as alcohol, were available.

More than 30,000 U.S. doctors served in the Army Medical Corps. Some of these men—women were not allowed in the corps—worked with British military doctors before the United States entered the war. They gained firsthand experience with battlefield medicine.

Mobile hospitals along the front lines were tents mired in mud. However, better facilities were found in base hospitals (off the battlefields), some of which were actually resort hotels. The U.S. Army and the Red Cross operated hospitals jointly,

Members of the American Army Medical Corps move a wounded man through ruins in Vaux, France.

and many of the nurses came from the Red Cross. The army relied on the Red Cross to provide oxygen and nitrous oxide ("laughing gas"). Nitrous oxide was a new anesthetic (pain killer) then, which the Red Cross described as "particularly valuable in cases where patients are too weak to take ether [a pain killer gas]."

Wounded soldiers were rushed to hospitals by the American Ambulance Field Service (later renamed the American Field Service) and other volunteer assistance groups. Ambulance drivers, who included hundreds of university students, as well as writers and artists, joined up through organizations based in the United States and Paris.

Only about 6 percent of wounded soldiers died of their wounds—a big reduction from previous wars. Nearly one-third of the men were treated for poison gas, which generally caused burns, long-term difficulties in breathing, and temporary blindness.

Five out of every six soldiers treated in hospitals because of battle wounds (including poison gas) returned to duty. Duty for these soldiers meant once again facing weapons that caused the death rate from battle to be higher than in any previous American war.

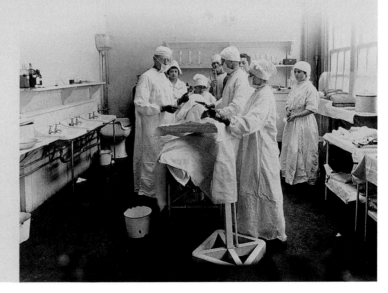

Doctors and nurses with a patient at a U.S. Army base hospital in Savenay, France

PERSHING'S ARMY

After the five German offensives failed, the Allied troops under Field Marshal Foch counterattacked with a vengeance. Foch planned for British and U.S. troops to squeeze the German army between giant pincers from the north and south, while the French troops pushed against the German lines from the center. The St. Mihiel Salient was in the U.S. sector.

As Foch's strategy became clear to him, German general Ludendorff began to pull his troops out of the St. Mihiel Salient on September 8, 1918. He wanted to concentrate German forces along part of the Hindenburg Line, Germany's most fortified set of trenches. Pershing did not know about Ludendorff's evacuation orders when he opened his attack on September 12.

Plenty of enemy troops were still in the area, and the doughboys were able to test their fighting skills. The Americans first shelled and gassed enemy positions for four hours. Then the newly formed U.S. Air Force attacked. Lieutenant Colonel William Mitchell—Pershing's chief aviation officer—directed about 1,500 planes. U.S. pilots flew 600 of them.

After the shelling stopped, the Yanks set a goal of advancing about 100 yards every four minutes. They encountered little resistance. In two days of fighting, the Americans captured the salient, about 13,000 German prisoners, and hundreds of artillery pieces.

As soon as the fighting at St. Mihiel Salient was over, the U.S. forces gathered to wage a campaign against German troops in the Argonne Forest, near the Meuse River. The Meuse-Argonne territory was vital to the Germans because it surrounded a railroad line that brought German troops, arms, and food into the southern half of the Western Front. A U.S. victory in this territory would severely cripple the enemy supply lines.

U.S. troops began a forced march of 50 to 100 miles to get to their sector of the Meuse-Argonne offensive. They were to capture the Meuse River area just north of Verdun and south of Sedan, as well as the Argonne Forest, about 24 miles west of the river.

Fifteen U.S. divisions were on the move. The Americans had never launched such a large military campaign. A convoy of 600,000 men, 90,000 horses, and thousands of trucks, tanks, big guns, and supply wagons slogged through the muddy, almost impassable roads. Some of the more distant divisions marched for a week. Horses died of starvation. Men died of exhaustion.

MEUSE-ARGONNE CAMPAIGNS

On September 25, most of the Americans were finally in place. They cut the wires that fastened tree branches to their big guns to hide them in the wooded area and opened fire. This time only 821 planes were available to help because the remaining ones supported Allied forces attacking elsewhere along the front. A rolling barrage from the big guns lobbed shells at the enemy over the heads of the advancing doughboys.

Within the first 48 hours, Pershing's troops took Montfaucon and the hill that dominated the area. But they were not able to capture the town and area surrounding Romagne a few miles north. German troops began reinforcing the area. By September 29, the U.S. advance stalled.

Soldiers cover their ears as a 14-inch gun launches a huge shell toward German troops in France's Argonne Forest, 1918.

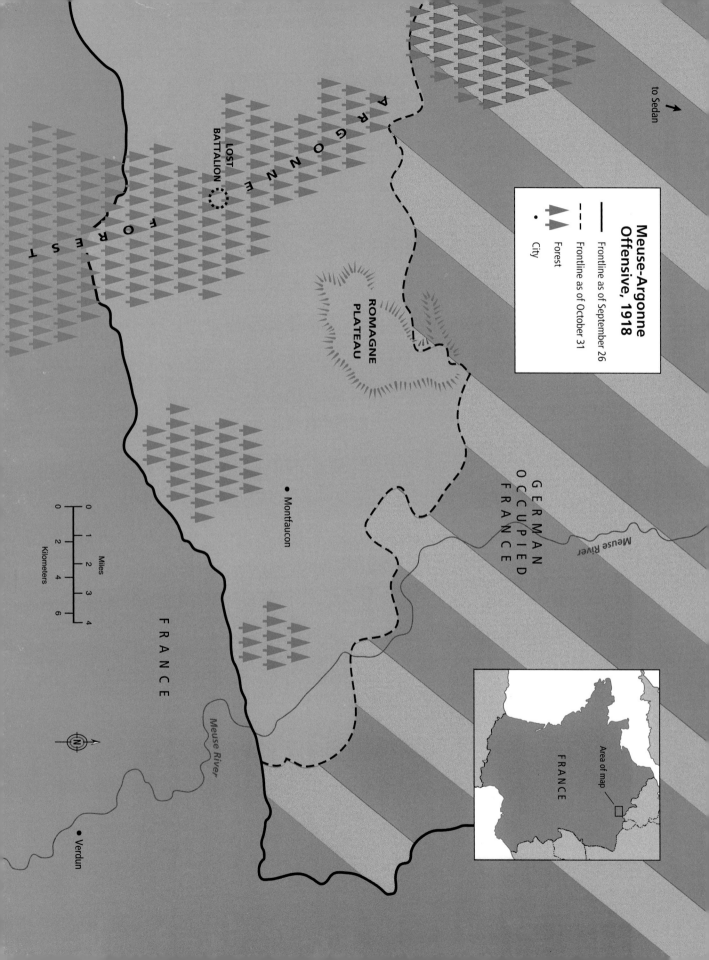

Meuse-Argonne
Offensive, 1918

Frontline as of September 26
Frontline as of October 31
Forest
City

to Sedan

A R G O N N E

LOST
BATTALION

F O R E S T

ROMAGNE
PLATEAU

Meuse River

GERMAN
OCCUPIED
FRANCE

Montfaucon

FRANCE

Miles
Kilometers

0 1 2 3 4
0 2 4 6

N

Meuse River

Verdun

FRANCE

Area of map

During September the U.S. troops still wore their summer uniforms, although the nights were getting cold. The doughboys were exhausted from constant shelling and gas attacks. Many had dysentery from drinking contaminated water. These were the conditions all soldiers on the Western Front had faced since September 1914. What was added in 1918 was influenza. This was not just the Spanish flu that spread during the previous spring, but a virus unlike any seen before.

The U.S. military reported that about 40 percent of its armed forces came down with the disease. The flu that plagued soldiers in Europe also hit troops and civilians in the United States. The story of Roscoe Vaughn is typical.

Private Vaughn, a 21-year-old soldier at Camp Jackson, South Carolina, reported to the army hospital on September 19. He had a cough and high fever and complained of chest pains. His lips and fingertips began to turn blue from lack of oxygen. No treatment seemed to work. By the early morning of September 26, Private Vaughn was dead. The army doctor conducted an autopsy. He saw that his patient—whose lungs were filled with fluid—had literally drowned.

The U.S. government canceled a draft call for 142,000 men, despite the need for more soldiers in Europe. By the first week in October, the deadly virus had spread worldwide, except for a few remote islands and Australia. About one-quarter of the people in

Frozen Flu

No one knows for sure where the 1918 strain of influenza virus came from or how it turned so deadly. In 1997 scientists traveled to a mass grave under the ice in a remote part of Alaska. They took tissue samples from the lungs of an Eskimo woman (with the permission of her relatives) who died of the flu in 1918. Because she was obese, the fat around her chest kept her lungs frozen. Other bodies in the grave had sometimes thawed and partially decayed. The virus in her lungs was still intact, giving scientists vital information they are using to figure out the mystery of why the flu was so deadly in 1918.

the United States caught the disease, and 500,000 died of it. Estimates of deaths around the globe range from 20 million to 100 million. The 1918 strain of flu killed more people within a span of several months than any other disease in recorded history, including the Black Plague.

The first week in October also marked a large loss of American lives in battle. About 26,000 doughboys were killed, and another 100,000 men were wounded as U.S. and German soldiers fought over every piece of ground in that densely wooded and rocky terrain in the Meuse-Argonne campaign.

Two events captured the imagination of the U.S. public during this campaign. One involved a group of soldiers from the 77th

EYEWITNESS QUOTE:
INFLUENZA!

"We have been averaging about 100 deaths a day. . . . For several days there were not enough coffins and the bodies piled up something fierce."

—An army doctor at Fort Devens, Massachusetts, September 29, 1918

Division that was surrounded by enemy troops for five days—Charles Whittlesey's Lost Battalion. Finally, other U.S. troops, including the 1st Division fighting just east of the forest, loosened the enemy's grip on the Argonne. At just about that time, Abraham Krotoshinsky, of the Lost Battalion, began his treacherous daylong crawl through enemy lines. Gassed and wounded, Private Krotoshinsky managed to get to American troops and lead them to his fellow soldiers. Of the 550 or so men of the Lost Battalion, only about 190 were able to walk out of the forest. At least 107 men had died, 190 were seriously wounded, and the rest were missing.

The other event concerned one of the soldiers responsible for driving Germans from the Argonne and thus helping Whittlesey's men. He was Alvin York, a religious mountainman from Tennessee. Legends sprang up about his exploits. As a

Sergeant Alvin York in the Argonne Forest near Cornay, France

sharpshooter protecting his squad, he likely killed about 20 German soldiers and captured 100 or more in one day. Corporal York was promoted to sergeant for his bravery.

While the Americans fought in the Argonne, Allied forces broke through Germany's Hindenburg Line. Field Marshal Foch was eager to continue Allied attacks on the retreating German army. He pressured Pershing to mount another campaign in the Meuse-Argonne area even though the American forces desperately needed to rest.

Pershing moved forward by planning a major offensive that started in a hilly area between Monfaucon and Romagne, where there was an important network of roads. Basically, the Americans started fighting again where they had stopped a few weeks before.

Pershing reorganized his troops. He created the Second U.S. Army headed by General Bullard and gave leadership of the First U.S. Army to Hunter Liggett. With two army-sized units to his military forces, Pershing became an army group commander. This gave him the same rank as Britain's General Haig and France's General Pétain.

The U.S. forces opened the new offensive on October 14. Their objective was to clear the Meuse-Argonne region of enemy troops and to cut the railroad line at Sedan. Pershing pushed his troops hard, advancing after every success.

The U.S. sector included territory along the Meuse River up to the town of Sedan, but not the town itself. Field Marshal Foch assigned capture of Sedan to the French,

The town of Sedan, France, 1918

because of the town's historic importance to France. In the Franco-Prussian War of 1870, Prussia (part of Germany) had captured France's emperor, Napoleon III, in Sedan. In that war, France gave up the French provinces of Alsace and Lorraine to Prussia.

By early November, some of Pershing's troops were close to Sedan. He wanted to take the town. The French military officers protested that the Americans were clogging the entry roads, so the French forces could not get through. A brief argument took place among the generals about how to proceed, but finally the American forces withdrew. French troops captured Sedan.

ARMISTICE

Weeks before the capture of Sedan, however, German general Ludendorff realized that victory in the Great War would go to the Allies. The Americans were fighting hard, and more of them kept coming. Germany, on the other hand, was on the edge of economic and political collapse.

Ludendorff met with his commander, Field Marshal Paul von Hindenburg. They agreed that it was time for Germany to seek an armistice—the end of fighting prior to a peace settlement. They hoped the armistice would allow the German army to return to the borders of Germany with enough strength to defend those borders.

The two men took their case to Kaiser Wilhelm, suggesting that Germany approach the Americans rather than France or Britain. They were suspicious that the European Allies wanted to weaken Germany. They hoped to make Wilson's Fourteen Points the basis for an armistice

Field Marshal Paul von Hindenburg (*left*) and **General Erich Ludendorff** (*right*) **tried to convince the kaiser to make the first move in the peace process.**

agreement. The kaiser wanted to keep his throne, and he was willing to put Germany in a position to meet Wilson's demands.

During the first week of October, Prince Maximillian von Baden (nicknamed Prince Max) became chancellor—the head of the Parliament in Germany and therefore head of the government. The kaiser agreed that only Parliament had the right to declare war or make peace. Making peace was just what Prince Max tried to do. On October 5, he sent a message to President Wilson. It read in part:

> The German Government requests the President of the United States to take a hand in the restoration of peace. . . . With a view to avoiding further bloodshed, the German Government requests the immediate conclusion of an armistice on land and water and in the air.

The next three weeks were filled with cautious negotiations between the United States and Germany. President Wilson ignored protests of the French and British leaders, whose troops had fought against the Central Powers four years longer than the Americans. He helped construct a new constitution for Germany and pushed for civilian rule. The kaiser remained on the throne, and Hindenburg retained his army, but General Ludendorff was forced to resign.

In late October, Edward House, Wilson's adviser, went to Paris to meet with Allied leaders. He tried to persuade them that the Fourteen Points and a Germany with enough strength left to negotiate reasonable terms offered Europe the best road to long-lasting peace.

Meanwhile, Field Marshal Foch met with Pershing, Pétain, and Haig. They agreed that Germany should be stripped of most of its military and railroad equipment. They wanted to create a neutral zone east of Germany's border at the Rhine River, extending 25 miles into German territory. Haig, Pétain, and Foch were in favor of armistice with these harsh terms. But Pershing, to his president's embarrassment, wanted even harsher terms. He wanted to push for Germany's unconditional surrender, with no concessions.

UNCONDITIONAL SURRENDER

Unconditional surrender means giving up to victorious enemy forces with no chance to negotiate favorable surrender terms.

FAST FACT

On November 1, 1918, the Hungarian government separated from Austria and left the war. On November 4, Austria signed an armistice with Italy. Germany stood alone against the Allies in the West.

With food supplies short and winter threatening, many Germans had had enough of war and enough of the kaiser. The Bolsheviks, the group who brought Communism to Russia, were working hard to bring a similar government to Germany. On November 7, about 20,000 German soldiers who had deserted from the front lines marched through the capital city of Berlin.

Prince Max had had enough too. That day he asked Field Marshal Foch to set up a meeting, and Foch agreed. So Foch, Admiral Sir Rosslyn Wemyss of the British Royal Navy, and several aides and interpreters set off by special train to a place in the woods near Compiègne, France. An equally small German delegation arrived the next morning.

As the German and Allied delegates began their talks on November 8, Communist-inspired forces seized control over part of the German navy. The uprising was put down by German army troops still loyal to the kaiser. On November 9, having lost the support of army and navy leaders, Kaiser Wilhelm II gave up his throne and fled to Holland.

By this time, the U.S. troops had finished their assigned mission of cutting the railroad line near Sedan. But General Pershing still wanted to go farther. On the night of November 10, two battalions of marines from the 2nd Division scrambled across footbridges over the Meuse River. They were met with German machine-gun fire. After some loss of life, they retreated.

That same night, the German delegation announced that they had not received an answer from their government, even though they had asked for instructions two days earlier. Field Marshal Foch stated that he had no authority to extend the armistice terms past 11:00 A.M. the next day, November 11.

The German delegation finally accepted the terms of the armistice, which included a German pullback from all occupied territory, and signed the agreement in the predawn hours of November 11. Pershing received word of the armistice by 6:00 A.M. but decided to continue fighting until the very last minute. U.S. troops occupied a few more towns and took positions on the east side of the Meuse River.

The armistice went into effect at the eleventh hour of the eleventh day of the eleventh month in 1918. President Wilson declared a holiday for government workers and announced to the nation: "The armistice was signed this morning. Everything for which America fought has been accomplished. It will now be our fortunate duty to assist by example, by sober, friendly counsel and by material aid in the establishment of a just democracy throughout the world."

Wilson and his wife celebrated by showing up unannounced at a ball given by the Italian Embassy in Washington. Then Wilson read from his Bible and went to bed.

MINORITIES IN WORLD WAR I

About 13,000 Native Americans served in World War I, even though the U.S. government didn't grant Native Americans citizenship until 1924. The most famous were Choctaw soldiers from Oklahoma. During the Meuse-Argonne Campaign, enemy soldiers often intercepted and broke coded messages the U.S. forces broadcast to each other. A U.S. commander overheard two of his Choctaw soldiers speaking in their native language. The three men came up with a way to use the Choctaw language as a code.

Other Choctaw soldiers were soon part of the experiment. Because the code was not mathematical or based on a language similar to anything the Germans knew, the Choctaw-coded messages were never broken. The Choctaw code talkers laid the foundation for the Navajo code talker program in World War II (1939–1945).

More than 200,000 African Americans served in World War I. But only about 11 percent of them were in combat forces. Most African Americans were put into labor units, loading cargo, building roads, and digging ditches.

African Americans served in segregated divisions (the 92nd and 93rd) and trained separately. The first training camp for black officers was set up at Fort Des Moines, Iowa. These men became the first black officers commissioned by the U.S. Army.

In some training camps, African Americans received little combat training and lived under poor conditions. During the winter of 1917–1918, some of the black

Major J. R. White and Lieutenant Colonel Otis B. Duncan—the two highest ranking African American officers in the U.S. Army during World War I—pose with Lieutenant W. J. Warfield (left to right). All three are members of the 369th Infantry Regiment.

Members of the all African American 369th Infantry Regiment

soldiers at Camp Alexander, Virginia, froze to death because they had no coats and slept in tents.

General Pershing wrote a letter—"Secret Information Concerning Black American Troops"—to French commanders leading African American soldiers. Reflecting an attitude common in the United States then, Pershing wrote: "Although a citizen of the United States, the black man is regarded by the white American as an inferior being. . . . The black is constantly being censured [criticized] for his want [lack] of intelligence and discretion, his lack of civic and professional conscience, and for his tendency toward undue familiarity. The vices of the Negro are a constant menace to the American who has to repress them sternly."

Ignoring Pershing's remarks, French field marshall Foch said he would welcome black troops. Pershing assigned the 369th Infantry Regiment (which was originally the 15th New York National Guard and was assigned to the all-black 93rd Division) to Foch. A 369th Regiment officer wrote: "Our great American general simply put the black orphan in a basket, set it on the doorstep of the French, pulled the bell, and went away. . . . The French were wonderful—wonderful—wonderful!"

The 369th fought more consecutive days than any other U.S. unit. When they weren't fighting, their band played jazz on tour in France. The band and the unit led New York's homecoming parade in February 1919.

UNEASY PEACE

An American newspaper reporter described the Western Front on November 11, 1918—Armistice Day—this way:

> For most of them, dirty and dog-tired in body and spirit, it was something unnatural, almost incredible. They stood up in trenches and cold wet foxholes, stretched themselves, looked about in wonderment, while, so close often that a stone would hit them, other figures stood up, too, and stretched themselves. They were gray-clad and had been enemies, whom our men had tried to kill, lest they themselves be killed.

For those who had survived, including about 204,000 wounded Yanks and count-less millions of wounded soldiers from other countries, it was time to go home. About 53,500 doughboys had died in battle, and another 63,000 had died from disease or other causes. These casualties were small compared to the estimated deaths suffered by Britain (900,000 men), France (1.4 million), Russia (1.7 million), and Germany and Austria-Hungary (3 million). The total civilian death toll was close to 25 million.

General Pershing created the Third U.S. Army—240,000 soldiers under Major General Joseph Dickman—to occupy U.S-held territory in Germany during treaty negotiations. Except for a small force in Russia, the First and Second Armies were to return to the United States as quickly as possible.

Although military battles were at an end, political conflicts were far from over. A peace conference was set for January 18, 1919, in Paris. President Wilson knew that it would be hard to convince Allied leaders to use the Fourteen Points as the basis for a peace treaty, so he decided to go to the conference in person.

In December Wilson sailed for France, the first U.S. president to leave the country while in office. Wilson brought along his wife and his personal doctor, Cary Grayson, as well as a delegation of advisers and more than 3,000 reports on issues that might come up during the negotiations.

After elections that fall, Republicans controlled the U.S. Congress. This would make it harder for a Democratic president to find the support needed in the Senate to ratify (approve) a peace treaty. Wilson did include one Republican on his negotiation team: retired diplomat Henry White. But

he did not invite Henry Cabot Lodge, who would head the Senate Foreign Relations Committee in the new Congress. If Lodge's committee did not recommend approval of the treaty, it was likely that the Senate as a whole would not ratify it.

Many European leaders gathered for the official opening of the peace conference at the French Foreign Office. But much of the important business was conducted by British prime minister David Lloyd George, French premier Georges Clemenceau, Italian premier Vittorio Orlando, and President Wilson, at Wilson's temporary mansion in Paris. These men were called the Council of Four or simply the Big Four. Russia, under its new Bolshevik government, did not take part in the peace conference.

President Wilson wanted to create a politically stable world in which a war such as the Great War would not happen again. And to do this, Wilson thought that the

British prime minister David Lloyd George, Italian premier Vittorio Orlando, French premier Georges Clemenceau, and U.S. president Woodrow Wilson (left to right) were nicknamed the Council of Four during the negotiations that ended World War I.

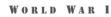

League of Nations (the fourteenth of his Fourteen Points) was the most important part of any plan for peace. He was willing to compromise on other areas as long as the League remained part of the treaty.

By the middle of February, Wilson could no longer stay away from the duties awaiting him back home. He returned to Washington.

One problem facing Wilson in Washington was mounting opposition to his League of Nations. Thirty-nine senators issued a statement that they would not ratify the proposed peace treaty. Most of these senators thought that the League interfered with the United States' ability to influence countries in the Western Hemisphere as outlined in the Monroe Doctrine.

The League was also under attack from nations at the peace conference who were more interested in weakening Germany and acquiring more territory than in creating lasting peace. When Wilson had returned to Washington in February, he had left his chief adviser, Edward House, in charge of representing the United States in the Paris treaty negotiations. When Wilson sailed back to Paris in mid-March, he discovered that House had negotiated away more than Wilson wanted him to. But the League of Nations provisions were still intact.

In the weeks to follow, Wilson tried to craft a treaty that would keep the main principles of the League of Nations and satisfy opponents of the League in the U.S. Senate. It was a difficult task.

When Wilson fell ill during April, his colleagues at the peace conference were not surprised. They knew he was under a lot of stress and that his health was fragile. But what they did not know then was that the president had suffered a small stroke. Wilson had high blood pressure. The headaches, weakness, and irritability he felt in April were likely due to a blood vessel that burst in his brain.

THE TREATY OF VERSAILLES

The treaty European leaders crafted in May (while Wilson was ill) was based on secret agreements made during the war rather than on Wilson's Fourteen Points. It contained more than 200 pages of harsh provisions for postwar Germany. Under the treaty, Germany lost about 13 percent of its territory in Europe and all of its colonies in other parts of the world.

The treaty also canceled the provisions of the Brest-Litovsk Treaty of 1918 that ended the fighting between Germany and Russia.

The Monroe Doctrine

In 1823 President James Monroe declared that the United States would protect all the countries of North, Central, and South America from interference by European countries. The United States used the Monroe Doctrine as a reason to send troops into neighboring countries, including Nicaragua and Haiti in 1915. Those countries had unstable governments. President Wilson wanted to ensure that European powers would not take advantage of the situation in Nicaragua to perhaps gain control of the recently opened Panama Canal. Only four years later, some Americans were concerned that President Wilson seemed to want to allow the League of Nations, rather than the United States, to decide what was best for Western Hemisphere countries.

Through that treaty, Germany had gained Russian-controlled Lithuania, Estonia, and Latvia. Under the terms of the new treaty, these three nations on the Baltic Sea became independent. Finland, which had separated from Russia in December 1917, was also recognized as an independent nation. The Polish people regained part of their own country, including access to the Baltic Sea. (Poland had been an independent kingdom, but in the late 1700s, Austria, Prussia, and Russia had each taken a part of the country, virtually wiping it off the map of Europe.)

Austria and Hungary became completely separate nations. Britain and France took control of much of the land in the Middle East that had been controlled by the Ottoman Empire (present-day Turkey), a supporter of Germany. The Arabs in these territories had fought for the Allies against the Ottomans, hoping to achieve independence after the war.

Serbia lost its independence as a result of the war. That country, which triggered the events leading to the Great War, became part of the newly formed group of southern European lands, including Bosnia-Herzegovina, called Yugoslavia.

Germany had to give up most of its military equipment, including its submarine fleet and many of its locomotives and railroad freight cars. The most severe provision of the treaty was Article 231, which required Germany to pay the Allies reparations, or money, for the cost of the war. These reparations included benefits to veterans and the families of soldiers killed in action. One estimate was that Germany would have to pay almost $100 billion.

In the spring of 1919, Germany was nearing economic collapse. The treaty demanded payments and conditions that Germany simply could not meet. Nevertheless, on June 28, 1919—five years after a Serbian nationalist killed Archduke Ferdinand and his wife—Germany signed the treaty in the Hall of Mirrors in the Palace of Versailles, France. After the Treaty of Versailles was signed, conference members drafted treaties for the other nations that had helped Germany. Turkish leaders

World leaders met in the Hall of Mirrors in the Palace of Versailles to discuss and sign the World War I peace treaty.

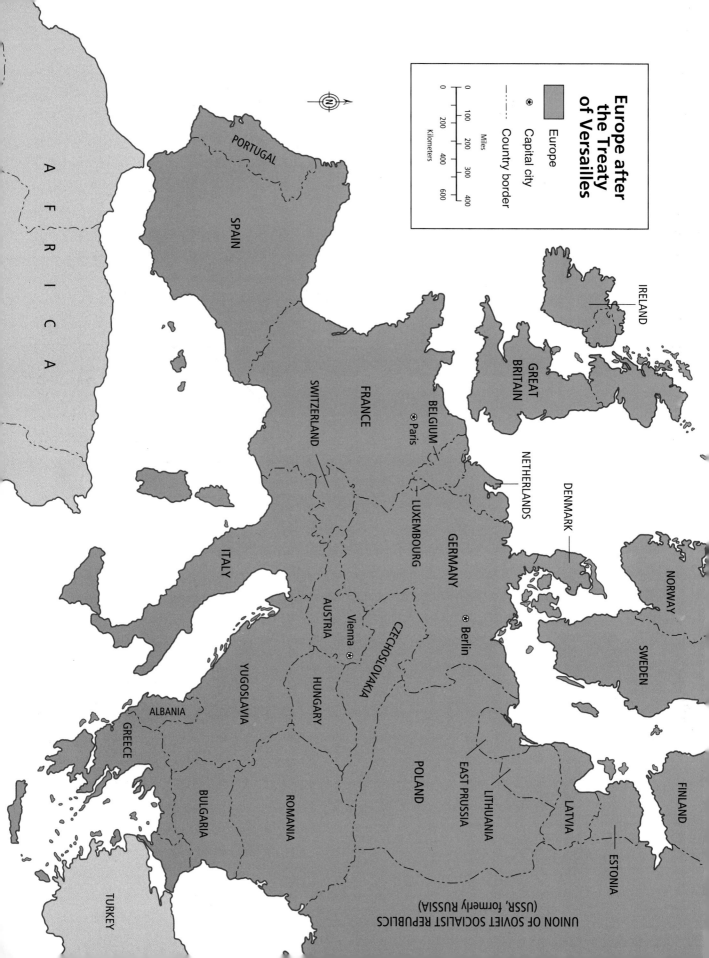

Europe after the Treaty of Versailles

Europe

⊛ Capital city

Country border

0   100   200   300   400
Miles

0   100   200   300   400   500   600
Kilometers

N

AFRICA

PORTUGAL

SPAIN

IRELAND

GREAT BRITAIN

SWITZERLAND

FRANCE

BELGIUM

⊛ Paris

NETHERLANDS

DENMARK

LUXEMBOURG

GERMANY

NORWAY

⊛ Berlin

SWEDEN

ITALY

AUSTRIA

Vienna
⊛

CZECHOSLOVAKIA

HUNGARY

POLAND

EAST PRUSSIA

LITHUANIA

LATVIA

FINLAND

ESTONIA

YUGOSLAVIA

ALBANIA

GREECE

BULGARIA

ROMANIA

TURKEY

UNION OF SOVIET SOCIALIST REPUBLICS
(USSR, formerly RUSSIA)

of the Ottoman Empire signed the last one, the Treaty of Sèvres, in August.

As soon as the Treaty of Versailles was signed, President Wilson prepared to leave for home. Harsh as the treaty was, it still contained a provision for the League of Nations. This new international organization would have an assembly of many nations of the world, but not Germany. The major world powers—Britain, France, Italy, Japan, and the United States—would form a council and cast deciding votes.

The German government ratified the Treaty of Versailles on July 7, just before Wilson reached American shores. As soon as he got back to the White House, Wilson went to work to convince Americans to ratify the treaty. It was a daunting task. The biggest hurdle was Henry Cabot Lodge, chairman of the Senate Foreign Relations Committee.

Nevertheless, Lodge accompanied the president when Wilson formally presented the Treaty of Versailles to the Senate. Wilson told senators: "[Peace] has come about by no plan of our conceiving, but by the hand of God who led us into this way. We cannot turn back. . . . The light streams upon the path ahead, and nowhere else."

But to Lodge and other senators, the path was not so clear. Most troublesome was Article 10 of the treaty, which required members of the League of Nations to pledge "to respect and preserve as against external aggression the territorial integrity [the current boundaries of the countries] and existing independence of all members of the League." Members were also bound by the decision of the League's Executive

Henry Cabot Lodge fought ferociously against the idea of a League of Nations.

Council. This wording seemed to threaten the United States' right to make its own decisions about foreign affairs.

On July 14, Lodge began to read every one of the treaty's 440 articles to the Senate. On the same day, Wilson began to hold 15-minute meetings with individual senators, to convince them of the worth of the treaty and the League of Nations. A few days later, Lodge was still reading the treaty (he took breaks!) when Wilson fell ill and had to postpone further meetings.

Wilson was willing to work with the Senate to ensure that the United States had the right to withdraw from the League of Nations and that the authority to declare war still rested with the U.S. Congress. But Wilson stood firm in his support of League members

protecting one another, an idea contained in Article 10. Without that, Wilson felt, the League of Nations "would be hardly more than an influential debating society."

At the end of July, the Senate Foreign Relations Committee began public hearings on the treaty. The League of Nations provisions continued to divide the president from the key senators needed to ratify the treaty. In August Lodge commented that he thought Wilson was "one of the most sinister figures that ever crossed the history of a great country."

WILSON'S FATEFUL TOUR

Determined to break the deadlock, President Wilson decided to take his arguments to the American people. In early September, he boarded his presidential train, the *Mayflower,* at Union Station in Washington, D.C. He headed for a whirlwind 8,000-mile tour of major cities throughout the Midwest and West to push hard for the treaty. Edith Wilson and a few other aides and advisers went too, along with the Secret Service and Dr. Grayson.

Wilson's headaches seemed to be more frequent and more severe. Buoyed by two days of well received speeches in

California, the president headed back East. By September 22, he complained of a splitting headache. On September 25, he gave a halting speech in Pueblo, Colorado, but pushed on for Wichita, Kansas. That night Wilson told his wife he felt sick. By the time Dr. Grayson saw him, Wilson was breathless and nauseous. The muscles in his face were twitching. Wilson commented to Joseph Tumulty, his personal secretary, "I seem to have gone to pieces."

One mile from Wichita that night, Tumulty ordered the tracks cleared for an emergency 1,700-mile race to the White House. Almost three days later the *Mayflower* rolled into Washington, D.C.

On October 2, 1919, President Wilson suffered a severe stroke. Only Edith

President Wilson *(center, in top hat)* **on his 1919 railroad tour of the United States**

Wilson, Dr. Grayson, and very few others were allowed at his bedside. The press was told that the president had had a nervous breakdown due to overwork and the flu but that his mind was alert.

"THE PRESIDENT SAYS . . . . "

Vice President Thomas Marshall waited for the Congress or the Supreme Court to order him to assume office during the president's illness. That order never came. Marshall was the first vice president to preside over a meeting of cabinet members (heads of executive departments) in the absence of the president. But it was Edith Wilson who actually took over much of the decision-making for her husband.

According to Mrs. Wilson, Dr. Francis Dercum, a specialist in nervous disorders, advised her to screen everything that would have gone to her husband and to consult with him only on matters she thought needed his advice. She said that Dr. Dercum told her it would hamper President Wilson's recovery and the postwar recovery of the nation if Wilson resigned.

Sometimes Joseph Tumulty or Secretary of State Lansing handled executive matters. But letters for the president went to Mrs. Wilson, who reviewed them and read some to her husband. She often replied herself on official White House stationery. The messages began with "The President says."

Meanwhile, senators continued to debate the pros and cons of topics that had led Wilson to make his cross-country tour—the Treaty of Versailles and the League of Nations. Senator Lodge drafted a compromise position and hoped to negotiate with Wilson on several complex matters in the

Edith Wilson

treaty. Lodge sent a note to the president, but he did not get a reply. It's not clear whether Wilson ever saw Lodge's note.

After several frustrating attempts to reach Wilson, Lodge drafted 14 reservations to the treaty. These reservations, an echo of Wilson's Fourteen Points, released the United States from some obligations under the treaty but kept membership in the League of Nations.

On November 6, the Senate Foreign Relations Committee approved the treaty as amended by Lodge. The committee sent the treaty to the full Senate for ratification. The senators debated with little guidance from the White House.

On November 19, the treaty with Lodge's reservations was ready to be voted on by the Senate. It failed to get the two-thirds majority needed for ratification. Then the Senate voted on the original version of the treaty. That, too, could not get a two-thirds majority. Because the Senate failed to ratify the treaty, the United States was still technically at war with the Central Powers. More importantly, Congress rejected Wilson's dream of the League of Nations and the peace that Wilson had crafted with his European allies.

President Wilson hardly slept the night after he learned of the Senate's vote. In the predawn hours, Wilson called for Dr. Grayson yet again. "Doctor," he said, "the devil is a busy man."

WOMEN IN WORLD WAR I

Female Red Cross nurses pose with army officers in front of a hospital in Milan, Italy.

Women were vital to the war effort. They went to work across the United States when millions of men became soldiers. Women took jobs in offices and factories and on farms. They drove trucks and managed businesses.

Women and women's organizations also supported the war directly. The National League for Women's Services and the Women's Committee of the Council of National Defense directed volunteer work. Women collected food, clothing, and books; made bandages; and supplied other goods for soldiers and needy civilians. The Women's Liberty Loan Committee sold Liberty Bonds and War Saving Stamps. "Four-Minute Women" addressed audiences in movie theaters. The Women's Land Army helped farmers.

Women helped U.S. troops through the Red Cross, the Salvation Army, and other organizations. These groups served coffee and doughnuts in canteens (military stores where soldiers could get refreshments and supplies) along the Western Front, helped soldiers write letters home, and volunteered to help care for the wounded in hospitals.

More than 16,000 civilian women worked overseas for the U.S. military. Most were nurses, clerical workers, and telephone operators. The Army Nurse Corps members wore uniforms but did not have military rank. The Army Medical Corps refused to admit female physicians. Women doctors from the United States served at the front anyway, often with the armed forces from Allied countries.

The law governing the U.S. Army referred to "male persons" as candidates for enlistment. But the U.S. Navy's law referred only to "persons." So Secretary of the Navy Josephus Daniels decided to open the U.S. Navy and Marine Corps to women. About 12,500 women performed office duties as clerical officers for the U.S. Navy, and 305 women did the same as members of the Marine Reserve.

On August 13, 1918, Opha Mae Johnson became the first woman enlisted in the Marine Corps Reserves. Johnson and other women aged 18 to 40 enlisted as privates (lowest rank) but could earn the higher rank of sergeant. Almost all of them worked at Marine Corps headquarters in Washington, D.C. At 7 A.M. daily, they reported to a field near the White House, where male instructors drilled them in standard parade maneuvers. These women practiced hard and were expected to be in top mental and physical condition. They were also top-notch secretaries. Nicknamed Lady Hell Cats and Marinettes, the women wore uniforms and received regular military pay and benefits. In 1919 the women marines were returned to civilian life in a ceremony on the White House lawn. The U.S. Navy's law was changed in 1925, closing enlistment to women.

At the end of World War I, most of the civilian jobs that had been filled by women during the war were taken back by returning soldiers. The main exceptions were jobs as secretaries and telephone operators. But one law—the Nineteenth Amendment to the Constitution—did profoundly change the role of women. Ratified on August 18, 1920, almost two years to the day after Opha Mae Johnson became a marine, the amendment stated that the right to vote shall not be denied or abridged by the United States or by an state on account of sex.

In a speech affirming a woman's right to vote, President Wilson said: "We have made women partners in the war; shall we admit them only to a partnership of suffering and sacrifice and toil and not to a partnership of privilege and right?" In 1920 women voted for president for the first time. Woodrow Wilson, who supported women's right to vote, was not on the ballot.

Enlisted navy women on the White House lawn. From 1918 to 1925, women were allowed to enlist in the U.S. Navy. In 1942, a law was passed that again allowed women to enlist.

EPILOGUE

By 1919 everyday life in the United States had changed. The Eighteenth Amendment had been added to the Constitution. When it went into effect in January 1920, the manufacture and sale of liquor was prohibited in the United States. Even the "girls back home" had changed. Women wore shorter skirts and smoked in public. The Nineteenth Amendment, which took effect in August 1920, gave women the right to vote.

African American soldiers who fought for Wilson's democratic principles in Europe wanted more equality at home. Membership soared in the National Association for the Advancement of Colored People (NAACP), which had been founded by blacks and whites in 1910. As 350,000 black veterans returned, their push for equality brought a backlash from some white Americans, particularly those in segregated southern states. Race riots in 1919 left scores of people dead. Some African American veterans, still in their army uniforms, were hung or burned to death.

TURBULENT TIMES

In April 1918, the newly created National War Labor Board (NWLB) had supported a shorter work week, equal pay for women, minimum wage standards, and the right to organize a labor union. Then the war ended suddenly and, in March 1919, so did the NWLB and its policies. Other government agencies and programs wound down after

The Illinois National Guard keeps the peace after race riots in Chicago in 1919.

grew to include about half the nation's steelworkers from Colorado to New York. Four months later, the strike officially ended with the workers admitting defeat.

At the same time, the success of the Communist revolution in Russia inspired some groups to try to bring similar changes to the United States. Most of these groups pushed for the social and economic reforms that were put forth before 1914 by the Progressive Party. But others wanted more radical change in the form of a Communist-style government, where all economic decisions are made by the government. In the summer of 1919, two U.S. Communist political parties were formed. (They would later join to become the American Communist Party.) Since labor unrest and strikes had led up to the Communist takeover in Russia, some Americans feared

the armistice too. Less funding was available for health- and child-care programs, housing programs, and assistance for lower-income people.

These changes resulted in turbulent times for working-class Americans. During 1919, labor strikes shook the nation. About 4.5 million workers—nearly one-quarter of the nation's labor force—walked off the job to strike for higher pay, shorter hours, and better working conditions. The first significant strike took place in Seattle, Washington, in February. About 60,000 workers throughout the city stopped work for five days, bringing transportation and industry to a standstill. Another major strike began on September 22, while Wilson was on his train tour. That strike

Graves's Men

Pressured by their allies, U.S. troops stayed in Russia until 1920. These soldiers, led by Major General William Graves, were sent to Siberia, the remote central and northeastern part of Russia, to prevent nearby Japan from invading and to rescue the Czech and Slovak armies. Graves's troops were caught up in the fighting of Russia's civil war, as Communists and non-Communists fought for control of the country. Some Americans were missing in action and were declared dead. Testimony before the U.S. Congress in 1991 revealed evidence that Russia kept some members of Graves's troops as prisoners. Some were freed in the 1920s and 1930s, but rumors remained that others were never released.

that people who pushed for reforms for U.S. workers might also be planning to overthrow the government. Hatred for Huns during the war turned to hatred of Reds (Communists) at war's end.

In August 1919, Attorney General Alexander Palmer created the General Intelligence Division (later renamed the Federal Bureau of Investigation), headed by a 24-year-old government lawyer, J. Edgar Hoover. Under Hoover's direction, the Department of Justice conducted raids to round up suspected Communist subversives (those working to overthrow the government) across the nation in 1919 and 1920. Nearly 10,000 people were arrested, and about 250 were deported (sent back) to Russia.

While the United States prepared to deport civilians to Russia, some U.S. troops were still in Europe waiting to come home. Since the November 1918 armistice, it had been a huge task to transport the two million Americans back to the United States. About 10,000 European women who had married doughboys were coming back to the United States too. In March 1919, a group of U.S. soldiers met in Paris and formed the American Legion to help returning war veterans. The group received its official name at a convention in the United States two months later.

The war also left about 6.5 to 8.5 million prisoners of war (POWs) on both sides. Few of them, probably about 4,000, were Americans. At the end of the war, the German army released prisoners all along the Western Front. These men, some of whom had been held in prison camps since 1914, struggled to find friendly troops and transportation back home. The U.S. Army did not release its prisoners until September 1919. The French army kept its prisoners even longer. Many of the POWs held by the French worked in factories, on farms, or on the railroads.

When the U.S. veterans did reach the United States, they were welcomed as heroes. General Pershing arrived to a huge victory parade in September 1919. He was

Why Dry?

World War I helped bring about the Prohibition era in the United States. During the war, U.S. grain went to feed soldiers rather than to produce liquor. Congress temporarily banned brewing and distilling. The Anti-Saloon League and the Women's Christian Temperance Union tried to persuade Congress to amend the Constitution to prohibit alcohol permanently, and they pressured state lawmakers to ratify the amendment. President Wilson vetoed the law (Volstead Act) that would enforce Prohibition, because he did not think the government should force moral values on individuals. But Congress overrode Wilson's veto, and Prohibition took effect on January 15, 1920. It was repealed in 1933.

U.S. soldiers who fought overseas in World War I march past the New York Public Library in a huge victory parade in 1918.

so popular that a campaign was launched to have him run for president. The African American members of the 369th Infantry Regiment marched in a New York City parade with their famous jazz band. Thousands cheered as they played a lively version of the French national anthem. With so many parades and so many veterans marching in them, entertainer Will Rogers joked: "We ought to let the boys sit in the grandstand and show our appreciation by marching past *them.*"

At the end of the war in 1918, about 3.7 million American soldiers remained, including those who had served in the United States. Each soldier discharged from service got an extra $60, his uniform, shoes, and a coat. Each soldier who had served in Europe also got to keep his helmet and gas mask. By the end of 1919, the U.S. Army had about 225,000 officers and men remaining on duty.

Those serving in Europe returned to a different country from one they had left a year or two before. Members of the American Legion post in Centralia, Washington, couldn't stand the recent labor unrest there and the threat of Communism on American soil. In November 1919, they marched on the local office of the International Workers of the World, a Communist-leaning labor

Boston Police gather Russian literature, which had been banned in an effort to prevent a Communist revolution in America. Starting after World War I, fear of a secret Communist movement caused the American government and public to discriminate against anyone with Communist beliefs.

organization. In the fight that followed, four Legion members were shot and several labor organizers were hung. This incident brought on violent attacks against labor groups all along the West Coast.

THE REST IS HISTORY

In December 1919, the White House issued a statement that President Wilson had "no compromise or concession of any kind in mind" regarding the Treaty of Versailles. Perhaps, he was too ill to hammer out an agreement that two-thirds of the Senate would accept. We'll never know.

The Allied nations, particularly Britain, made it clear that they were eager for U.S. participation in the League of Nations on almost any terms. But Article 10 remained a sticking point. A group of senators tried to find a compromise without help from President Wilson. In March 1920, the Senate tried once again to ratify the Treaty of Versailles and failed. That year more than 40 nations founded the League of Nations in Geneva, Switzerland. The League was based on the pledges that Wilson helped to draft, but the United States never agreed to become part of it.

On April 14, 1920, President Wilson met with his cabinet for the first time in seven months. He seemed unaware of current issues and had little to say. He continued to focus on the one goal that seemed impossible for him to accomplish—American membership in the League of Nations. Despite his weakened state, Wilson wanted a third term as president. With four more years, so he reasoned, he could show the American public the wisdom of joining the League.

Wilson tried to convince the Democratic National Convention. But the convention delegates chose James Cox to be their presidential candidate and Franklin Delano Roosevelt to be his running mate. Wilson did little to support Cox directly. Americans chose Republican candidate Warren Harding and his running mate Calvin Coolidge by 61 percent of the vote. They also voted Republicans into the majority of seats in Congress.

On December 10, 1920, President Wilson received the 1919 Nobel Peace Prize for his efforts to establish the League of Nations and for trying to bring a just end to the Great War. He stayed in the White House until the end of his term in March 1921, then moved to a house at 2340 S Street NW, in Washington, D.C.

The Great War formally ended on July 2, 1921, when Congress passed a joint resolution that declared that hostilities with Germany, Austria, and Hungary were over. The Senate ratified peace treaties with these countries on July 18. The last of the U.S. soldiers left Germany in 1923. Former president Wilson continued to press for U.S. membership in the League of Nations until just days before his death on February 3, 1924. His opponent on this issue, Senator Henry Cabot Lodge, died later that year.

In 1923 an Austrian veteran of the Great War was arrested and convicted of treason. He had led about 2,000 members of the National Socialist German Workers (Nazi) Party in a raid against government offices in the German state of Bavaria. In December 1924, he was released from prison after serving a short sentence. While in prison, he had started writing *Mein Kampf* (*My Struggle*), which included plans to regain land Germany lost in the Treaty of Versailles. The soldier's name was Adolf Hitler.

Cher Ami, the carrier pigeon that helped save the Lost Battalion, is with us to this day. Medics made him an artificial leg to replace the one shot off while flying to headquarters. Cher Ami was retired from active duty and died about a year later. He was stuffed and sent to the Smithsonian Institution, in Washington, D.C. Cher Ami remains there with his Croix de Guerre (Cross of War), a war-service medal France awarded to him for bravery.

A few months after the United States formally ended hostilities, the war claimed another life. Charles Whittlesey, who received many honors for leading the Lost Battalion, could not forgive himself for the suffering he imposed on his men in the Argonne Forest. After attending an Armistice Day ceremony in 1921, Major Whittlesey put his business affairs in order. He boarded a ship for Cuba, wrote letters to friends and relatives, left a note for the ship's captain, and jumped overboard.

After the United States rejected the Treaty of Versailles, the *New York Times* had predicted that "the real League of Nations will come after the next war." The newspaper editors were right. In 1946, shortly after World War II was over, the League of Nations formally ended and the United Nations took its place. Edith Wilson lived to see the United States participate in this international organization, which works to bring peace to nations the world over and which would probably would have satisfied both her husband and Senator Lodge.

EYEWITNESS QUOTE:
VENGEANCE

"It cannot be that two million Germans should have fallen in vain. . . . No, we cannot pardon, we demand—vengeance!"

—Adolf Hitler,
September 18, 1922

MAJOR BATTLES OF WORLD WAR I – THE WESTERN FRONT

Battle of the Marne	September 5–September 14, 1914
Ypres	October–November 1914
Verdun	February 21–July 1916
Battle of the Somme	July 1–November 1916
Somme River Offensive	March 21–April 1918
Cantigny	May 27–May 28, 1918
Château-Thierry	June 1918
Belleau Wood	June 6–June 25, 1918
Second Battle of the Marne	July 15–August 1918
St. Mihiel Salient	September 12–September 13, 1918
Meuse-Argonne Campaign	September 26–November 11, 1918

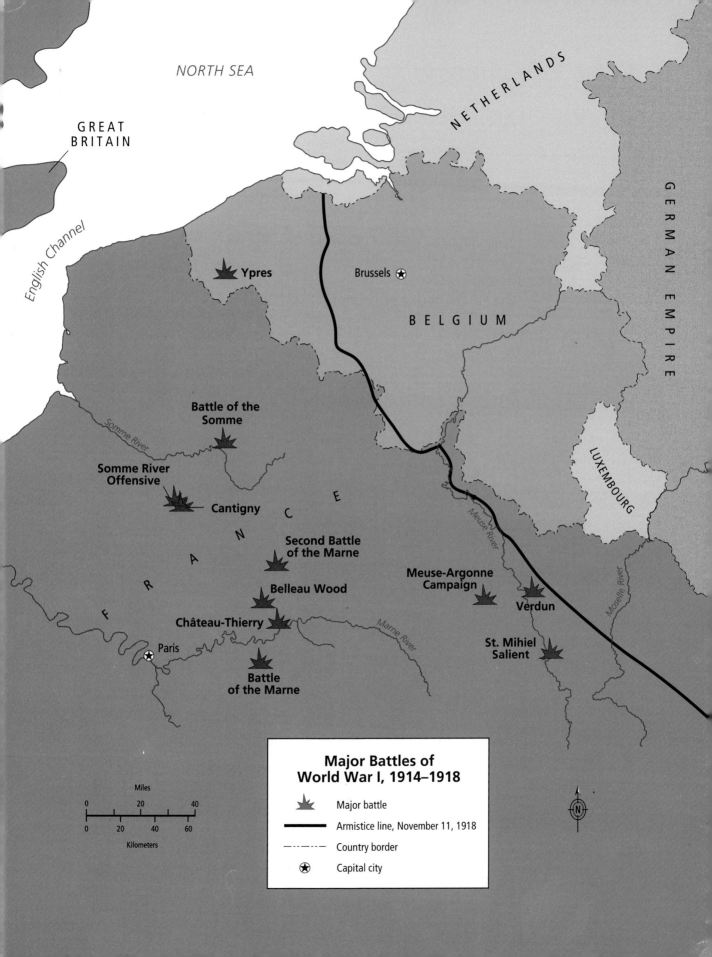

NORTH SEA

GREAT
BRITAIN

English Channel

NETHERLANDS

GERMAN EMPIRE

★ Ypres

Brussels ✪

BELGIUM

LUXEMBOURG

Somme River

**Battle of the
Somme**

**Somme River
Offensive**

Cantigny

F R A N C E

**Second Battle
of the Marne**

Meuse River

**Meuse-Argonne
Campaign**

Belleau Wood

Château-Thierry

Marne River

Verdun

Moselle River

Paris ✪

**St. Mihiel
Salient**

**Battle
of the Marne**

Major Battles of
World War I, 1914–1918

★ Major battle

▬▬▬ Armistice line, November 11, 1918

–·–·–· Country border

✪ Capital city

Miles
0   20   40

0   20   40   60
Kilometers

N

WORLD WAR I TIMELINE

1914	Serbia nationalist kills Austrian archduke and duchess in Sarajevo, Bosnia-Herzegovina, on June 28.
	Austria-Hungary declares war on Serbia on July 28.
	Germany declares war on Russia, and France and invades Belgium.
	Britain declares war on Germany on August 4.
	U.S. president Woodrow Wilson declares U.S. neutrality on August 19.
	Battle of the Marne begins on September 5.
	Battle of Ypres begins in October and lasts through November
1915	Jane Addams helps form the Woman's Peace Party in January.
	Britain begins blockade of goods into Germany on March 1.
	German submarine sinks the ocean liner *Lusitania* on May 7.
1916	Battle of Verdun begins on February 21.
	Battle of the Somme lasts from July through November.
	President Wilson wins reelection on November 7.
1917	Revolution in Russia drives czar from the throne in March.
	United States declares war on Germany on April 6.
	First U.S. troops arrive in France on June 26.
1918	Wilson issues Fourteen Points plan for peace on January 8.
	Somme River Offensive begins on March 21.
	Battle of Cantigny lasts from May 27 to May 28.
	Battle of Chateau-Thierry begins in June.
	Battle of Belleau Wood begins on June 6.
	Second Battle of the Marne lasts from July through August.
	Fighting at the St. Mihiel Salient lasts from September 12 to September 13.
	U.S. forces launch Meuse-Argonne Campaign on September 26.
	Armistice is signed on November 11.
1919	Warring parties sign Treaty of Versailles on June 28.
	Wilson suffers stroke on October 2.
	Senate rejects Treaty of Versailles on November 19.
1921	U.S. Congress declares war with Germany and Austria-Hungary is over on July 2.

GLOSSARY

armistice: temporary end to fighting by a formal agreement of the warring parties

artillery: mounted guns. Artillery can be light or heavy, depending on the size of the gun shells that are fired.

blockade: shutting off an area with troops or ships in order to prevent the free-flowing passage of goods

casualties: members of the armed forces who are lost to active service because they have been wounded, killed, or captured

doughboy: slang for a U.S. soldier. This name was particularly popular in World War I.

Hindenburg Line: known to Germany as the Siegfried Line. This was a series of fortified trenches built by the Germans in 1916 and 1917 across northern France and Belgium.

League of Nations: international organization established in 1920 to maintain peace among countries around the world. The United States did not join, and Germany was not allowed to join. The League was replaced by the United Nations after World War II.

poison gas: vaporized chemicals used to weaken, kill, or immobilize soldiers. The three most commonly used gases in World War I were mustard gas, chlorine gas, and phosgene gas.

salient: an area of land that bulges out from the main battle lines into enemy territory and is difficult to defend

trench warfare: a type of battle in which opposing armies dig defensive ditches or bunkers connected by ditches. World War I soldiers lived in and worked from the trenches. In battle, they went "over the top" of their trenches, raced across "no-man's land" (the area separating the two opposing sides, that is claimed by neither) and attacked soldiers in enemy trenches.

U-boat: German submarine. U-boat stands for *unterseeboot*, which is German for "undersea boat."

Western Front: in World War I, the forward line of battle between the German and Allied forces in France and Belgium. This front, which was fortified with trenches, was west of Germany.

WHO'S WHO?

Newton Diehl Baker (1871–1937)

Newton Baker was a lawyer and the mayor of Cleveland, Ohio, when Wilson asked him to be secretary of war. Baker was a progressive Democrat who pushed for social reforms and supported antiwar organizations. Many were surprised when he accepted the job. Baker refused to appoint General Leonard Wood, a tough militarist, to lead the American Expeditionary Force. As a result, he was severely criticized by Republican leaders, such as Henry Cabot Lodge. Baker assembled four million U.S. troops, toured the front lines with General Pershing, and helped draw up the plans of the League of Nations. In 1920 he returned to practicing law and later joined the Permanent Court of Arbitration, an international court at The Hague in the Netherlands.

Eugene Jacques Bullard (1894–1961)

Born in Georgia, Eugene Bullard left home at age eight. Bullard went to Paris in 1913 as a boxer, joined the French army, and flew in the French Flying Corps. He was the first black man in the world to become a fighter pilot. When the newly formed U.S. Air Force did not respond to his application to join, Bullard continued to fly for France. After the war, Bullard opened a jazz nightclub in Paris. He then returned with his daughters to the United States and became an elevator operator. Bullard was buried with full French military honors in Flushing, New York.

Jane A. Delano (1862–1919)

After serving as a volunteer nurse in the Spanish-American War (1898), Jane Delano taught nursing and became the superintendent of the Army Nurse Corps. A native of Townsend, New York, she also founded the Red Cross Nursing Corps. When the United States entered World War I, she coordinated the activities of the Army Nurse Corps and the nurses in the American Red Cross. She recruited most of the American nurses who served with the army during the war. In 1919 Delano died of an infection while touring military hospitals in France.

Erich Ludendorff (1865–1937)

Born near Posen, Germany (present-day Poznan, Poland), Erich Ludendorff started military training at age 12. Ludendorff worked extremely hard and became a brilliant soldier, rising to the rank of general. He was second in command to Paul von Hindenburg. The two men defeated the Russians on the Eastern Front. They ran Germany as a military dictatorship in 1918, but when they lost on the Western Front, Ludendorff was forced to resign and later fled to Sweden.

Mata Hari (1876–1917)

Born Margaretha Geertruida Zelle to a middle-class family in the Netherlands, Mata Hari married a Dutch army officer and went to Java in the South Pacific. She later returned to Europe alone and penniless. Using her striking beauty and her Malay nickname, Mata Hari, she became an exotic dancer. She was known for her snake dances, which she fashioned after those she had seen in Java. During World War I, she had affairs with men on both sides of the war. The French accused her of spying for Germany, although some historians think that she was set up by the Germans as part of a trap. Mata Hari was convicted of causing the death of more than 50,000 Allied soldiers and was executed by a French firing squad in 1917.

John Joseph Pershing (1860–1948)

Before leading the American Expeditionary Force in Europe, John Pershing attended West Point military academy in New York, fought in the Spanish-American War (1898), and led U. S. forces in search of Pancho Villa in Mexico. Pershing's house in California burned down while Pershing was away in August 1915, and his wife and three daughters died in the fire. Only Pershing's son, who was also away, survived. During the bloody battles of 1918, Pershing once broke down in tears and said to his driver: "My God, I sometimes wonder if I can go on."

Jeanette Rankin (1880–1973)

Jeanette Rankin was the first woman elected to the U.S. Congress. One of the first votes she cast involved U.S. entry into World War I. "I want to stand by my country," she said, "but I cannot vote for war. I vote No." A Republican from Montana, Rankin served in the House of Representatives from 1917 to 1919, before women had the right to vote in national elections. She was later reelected to Congress and was the only member of the House to vote against U.S. entry into World War II.

Manfred von Richthofen (1892–1918)

Born in Breslau, Germany (present-day Wroclaw, Poland), Manfred von Richthofen attended military academies and loved hunting as a young man. When World War I began, he was already part of the German cavalry. But a cavalryman has little to do in trench warfare, so Richthofen joined the German air force and became an ace (outstanding) fighter pilot. He painted his Fokker triplane bright red, from which came his nickname, the Red Baron. Richthofen shot down 80 enemy planes before he was shot down in a dogfight with a British pilot over the Somme River in France.

SOURCE NOTES

4 Merion Harries and Susie Harries, *The Last Days of Innocence: America at War, 1917–1918* (New York: Random House, 1997), 374.

5 June A. English and Thomas D. Jones, *Scholastic Encyclopedia of the United States at War* (New York: Scholastic, Inc., 1998), 102.

5 John S. D. Eisenhower, *Yanks: The Epic Story of the American Army in World War I* (New York: The Free Press, 2001), 237.

5 L. C. McCollum, "History and Rhymes of the Lost Battalion," *Brigham Young University Library*, n.d. <http://www.lib.byu.edu/~rdh/wwi/memoir/Lost/LostBatTC.htm> (October 6, 2003).

5 Ibid.

13 August Heckscher, *Woodrow Wilson: A Biography* (New York: Charles Scribner's Sons, 1991), 339.

13 John Milton Cooper Jr., *Pivotal Decades: The United States, 1900–1920* (New York: W. W. Norton & Company, 1990), 221.

13 Heckscher, 341.

16 Robert H. Zieger, *America's Great War: World War I and the American Experience* (Lanham, MD: Rowman & Littlefield Publishers, 2000), 22.

16 Cooper, 234.

24 Ibid., 250.

25 Ibid., 256.

25 Ibid., 258.

25 Ibid.

25 Ibid., 259.

25 Ibid.

26 English and Jones, 97.

26 Heckscher, 431.

27 Phyllis Lee Levin, *Edith and Woodrow: The Wilson White House* (New York: Charles Scribner's Sons, 2001), 177.

28 Zieger, 53.

28 Levin, 178.

28 Harries, 71.

28 Frances Early, *A World without War: How U.S. Feminists and Pacifists Resisted World War I* (Syracuse, NY: Syracuse University Press, 1997), 3.

29 Zieger, 79.

29 Eisenhower, 41.

32 Harries, 94.

33 Levin, 180.

34 Harries, 159.

34 Ibid.

35 David McCullough, *Truman* (New York: Simon & Schuster, 1992), 103.

35 Eisenhower, 53.

35 Michael E. Hanlon, "The Origins of Doughboy," *Great War Society*, June 16, 2003, <http://www.worldwar1.com/dbc/origindb.htm> (October 6, 2003).

39 Harries, 220.

39 Ibid.

39 Byron Farwell, *Over There: The United States in the Great War, 1917–1918* (New York: W.W. Norton & Company, 1999), 302.

42 Eisenhower, 114.

44 Harries, 295.

45 Ibid., 158.

46 Eisenhower, 145.

48 Ibid., 161.

48 Zieger, 98.

48 Eisenhower, 174.

51 Red Cross War Council, *The Work of the American Red Cross during the War: A Statement of Finances and Accomplishments for the Period July 1, 1917 to February 28, 1919.* (Washington, D.C.: American Red Cross, October 1919), 54.

55 Gina Kolata, *Flu: The Story of the Great Influenza Pandemic of 1918 and the Search for the Virus That Caused It* (New York: Farrar, Straus and Giroux, 1999), 14.

58 Eisenhower, 244.

59 Levin, 222.

61 Gail Buckley, *American Patriots: The Story of Blacks in the Military from the Revolution to Desert Storm* (New York: Random House, 2001), 163.

61 Ibid., 202.

62 Zieger, 284.

67 Heckscher, 582.

67 Zieger, 179.

68 Levin, 314.

68 Ibid., 311.

68 Ibid., 331.

69 Ibid., 335.

69 Heckscher, 631.

70 Ibid., 629.

71 Cooper, 308.

75 Farwell, 286.

77 Levin, 414.

77 John Keegan, *The First World War* (New York: Alfred A. Knopf, 1999), 3.

83 English and Jones, 104.

83 Harries, 72.

SELECTED BIBLIOGRAPHY, FURTHER READING, & WEBSITES

SELECTED BIBLIOGRAPHY

Buckley, Gail. *American Patriots: The Story of Blacks in the Military from the Revolution to Desert Storm.* New York: Random House, 2001.

Cooper, John Milton Jr. *Pivotal Decades: The United States, 1900–1920.* New York: W. W. Norton & Company, 1990.

Cornebise, Alfred E. *War As Advertised: The Four Minute Men and America's Crusade, 1917–1918.* Philadelphia: The American Philosophical Society, 1984.

Eisenhower, John S. D. *Yanks: The Epic Story of the American Army in World War I.* New York: The Free Press, 2001.

Farwell, Byron. *Over There: The United States in the Great War, 1917–1918.* New York: W. W. Norton & Company, 1999.

Harries, Merion, and Susie Harries. *The Last Days of Innocence: America at War, 1917–1918.* New York: Random House, 1997.

Heckscher, August. *Woodrow Wilson: A Biography.* New York: Charles Scribner's Sons, 1991.

Hewitt, Linda L. *Women Marines in World War I.* Washington, D.C.: U.S. Marine Corps, 1974.

Keegan, John. *The First World War.* New York: Alfred A. Knopf, 1999.

Kolata, Gina. *Flu: The Story of the Great Influenza Pandemic of 1918 and the Search for the Virus That Caused It.* New York: Farrar, Straus and Giroux, 1999.

Levin, Phyllis Lee. *Edith and Woodrow: The Wilson White House.* New York: Charles Scribner's Sons, 2001.

Red Cross War Council. *The Work of the American Red Cross during the War: A Statement of Finances and Accomplishments for the Period July 1, 1917 to February 28, 1919.* Washington, D.C.: American Red Cross, October 1919.

Stackelberg, Roderick. *Hitler's Germany.* London: Routledge, 1999.

Zeiger, Susan. *In Uncle Sam's Service: Women Workers with the American Expeditionary Force, 1917–1919.* Ithaca, NY: Cornell University Press, 1999.

Zieger, Robert H. *America's Great War: World War I and the American Experience.* Lanham, MD: Rowman & Littlefield Publishers, 2000.

FURTHER READING

Adams, Simon. *World War I.* New York: Dorling Kindersley, 2001.

Dommermuth-Costa, Carol. *Woodrow Wilson.* Minneapolis: Lerner Publications Company, 2003.

English, June A., and Thomas D. Jones. *Scholastic Encyclopedia of the United States at War.* New York: Scholastic, 1998.

Marrin, Albert. *The Yanks Are Coming: The United States in the First World War.* New York: Atheneum, 1986.

Prendergast, Tom, and Sara Prendergast. *World War I: Almanac.* New York: U-X-L, 2002.

———. *World War I: Biographies.* New York: U-X-L, 2002.

———. *World War I: Primary Sources.* New York: U-X-L, 2002.

Winter, Jay, and Blaine Baggett. *The Great War and the Shaping of the 20th Century.* New York: Penguin Studio, 1996.

WEBSITES

First World War.com. This comprehensive World War I resource provides online battlefield tours, photos and descriptions of weapons, and countless editorials on key players, battles, and the aftermath of the Great War. Be sure to check out the Vintage Audio link.
<http://www.firstworldwar.com/>

Great War in the Air. This online exhibit explores the importance of World War I air combat.
<http://www.nasm.si.edu/galleries/gal206/gal206.html>

The Great War and the Shaping of the 20th Century. Based on an eight-part PBS television series on World War I, this website includes timelines, maps, and interviews with prominent historians.
<http://www.pbs.org/greatwar/>

The Women Veterans Historical Project. This online World War I exhibit includes photos and information about female doctors, nurses, and soldiers who participated in the war effort.
<http://library.uncg.edu/depts/archives/exhibits/Veterans/wwI.html>

The World War I Document Archive. This searchable database of treaties, speeches, and personal letters also contains a photo section and biographical dictionary.
<http://www.lib.byu.edu/~rdh/wwi/>

INDEX

ABOUT THE AUTHOR

Ruth Tenzer Feldman is an award-winning author, whose works include a biography of Thurgood Marshall, *How Congress Works, Don't Whistle in School: The History of America's Public Schools, The Mexican-American War,* and *The Korean War.* A former attorney with the U.S. Department of Education, Ms. Feldman is also a frequent contributor to *Cobblestone* and *Odyssey* magazines. She shares her Bethesda, Maryland, home with her family, her Welsh corgi, and her trusty computer.

PHOTO ACKNOWLEDGMENTS

The images in this book are used with the permission of: National Archives, pp. 4, 8, 14, 18, 19, 22 (both), 23, 24, 26 (top), 32, 33 (both), 35, 38 (center), 40, 42, 47, 50, 51 (top), 56, 60, 61, 62, 63, 65, 75, 82 (bottom), 83 (second from top), 83 (bottom); Kodia Photo and Graphics, p. 6; Library of Congress, pp. 7, 15, 17, 28, 29, 34, 45, 67, 69, 70, 71, 82 (top); Laura Westlund, pp. 9, 20, 41, 43, 49, 54, 66, 79; © Bettmann/CORBIS, pp. 10, 44, 57, 58, 72; State Historical Society of Colorado, p. 12; Dictionary of American Portraits, p. 13; Trustees of the Imperial War Museum, p. 16; Illustrated London News, pp. 21, 27; © CORBIS, pp. 26 (bottom), 36, 52, 53, 82 (second from bottom), 83 (second from bottom); © Hulton-Deutsch Collection/CORBIS, pp. 30, 38 (top and bottom), 76; © Underwood & Underwood/CORBIS, pp. 11, 37; © Hulton | Archive by Getty Images, p. 46; National Library of Medicine, p. 51 (bottom); Woodrow Wilson Collection, Seeley G. Mudd Manuscript Library, Princeton University Library, p. 68; Chicago Historical Society, p. 73; Bentley Historical Library, University of Michigan, p. 74; U.S. Air Force, p. 82 (second from top); Independent Picture Service, p. 83 (top).

Cover: © Corbis.